ACE AT WORK

Exploring Nuances of Career Growth & Fulfilment

By Pragnya Venigalla

INDIA • SINGAPORE • MALAYSIA

ISBN 979-8-89186-974-5

Dedication

To my *Sister*, *Soujanya*, who knowingly or unknowingly has helped shape the way I show up and think about work and life!

Contents

Acknowledgements

I extend my deepest gratitude to all my loved ones for supporting me in the journey of writing this book.

- My Mother, who never stopped believing in me!
- My Father, who unquestionably stood as my anchor!
- My Sister, with whom I would bicker and have deep conversations, always pushed me to think differently!
- My husband, Praveen, for all his love and unwavering support throughout this process!
- My son, Pradyut, who continues to test me and question the way I look at the world!

Kiruba Shankar, a fellow member of PSAI (Professional Speakers Association of India), signed his book for me with the words: "Dear Peggy, look forward to buying your first book. Thank you for inspiring me with your enthusiasm." Up until that point, the thought of writing a book had never crossed my mind. To Kiruba, for sowing the seed for this book and being a mentor whom I look up to, I am forever grateful! I would also like to take this opportunity to thank PSAI and its members for reinforcing the belief that I too can write a book.

Chimmu Kutty and Navneetha Lokanathan, my friends, confidants, and supporters, deserve a special mention as they have played a phenomenal role in the outcome of this book.

This book would not have been possible if not for the experiences of working with all my colleagues, clients, and mentors. Each of them has helped me by teaching valuable lessons that are explored in this book.

Thank you for all the love and support!

Introduction

As someone who has heard the request "I need a job" countless times, I am constantly surprised by it for three things – the audacity, the lack of clarity, and the casualness of the request. Let me explain!

I am often amazed by the audacity of people who approach me with this request without knowing me or my connections, expecting me to hand them a job. However, my problem with this statement extends beyond the lack of opportunity I can provide; it also stems from the fact that I may or may not know this person well enough!

I also find it frustrating that many people don't seem to understand what they are really looking for. With so many job possibilities out there, the "I need a job" request is so vague without a follow-up comment clarifying what job! It's impossible to know what kind of job someone is seeking or what their qualifications are without any information. And how can I or anyone even think of helping without this basic information? It's essential to know what type of job best fits your qualifications, experience, and interests. And yet, so many people approach the job search with a "one size fits all" mentality, expecting anyone and everyone to be able to help them.

The reality is that a job is much more than just a three-letter word. It's something that consumes a significant portion of our lives, and yet many of us don't give it the attention it deserves. As someone who has spent over a decade in corporate settings and who has experience as a freelancer and entrepreneur, I've been guilty of and seen firsthand the lack of importance we give to our work and, more importantly, the effect it has on the rest of our lives.

It's a lifestyle that we all too easily fall into, one that leaves us feeling stuck in a monotonous cycle of waking up, going to work, and waiting for the weekend! Our jobs have become mundane, and we lack excitement in our lives. We are often left with a feeling of "there has to be something more to life" and many times, question what we are doing! We feel trapped - In jobs where we feel underappreciated and bored; in difficult environments that make us stressed, anxious, and depressed; in lives that feel out of control!

If this sounds familiar to you, I invite you to join me on a journey to break free from this cycle, and it starts with changing our relationship with work. Being a recovering workaholic myself, I truly understand where you are and what you are going through! I have been there too, and honestly, find myself there from time to time! But I know my way out now! In this book, I unveil what I have compiled from my own experiences, observing people, and working with coaching clients. Whether you are looking to change jobs, get promoted and grow in your career, make more money, or are just looking to enjoy your work and feel fulfilled, the key is this – Ace at work. In this book, I aim to decode how we can do just that. By tackling this significant aspect of our lives, we can experience true meaning and live more fully.

By becoming an Ace at work, we can take back control of our career growth and lives and stop allowing work to seep into every aspect of our existence. It's not about working harder or squeezing every last drop out of our day but rather about managing ourselves and our work more effectively. These are the nuances that aid in our career growth and fulfilment.

This book is written in three parts, each outlining an aspect of the foundational idea of Ace At Work – **Awareness, Change, and Excel.** It is recommended to go through these in the same order to make the most of the book. It is a step-by-step blueprint that takes you through the different phases needed to change the way we work.

> **Part 1** talks about building AWARENESS about ourselves at work – what we do and how we do it! It is only when we truly understand this that we can be honest about where we want to go!
>
> **Part 2** talks about the CHANGE we can make in the way we work to fuel us in our journey. We walk through mindset shifts and activities that help us on the stepping stones on our journey.
>
> **Part 3** takes us through tools and techniques we can implement to EXCEL at work and accelerate our career growth. This is what makes our 'job' more than what it is!

The A.C.E. Blueprint will serve you well, to build fulfilling lives, just like it has helped me and my coaching clients. If you are honest with yourself, do the exercises, and implement the tools and techniques outlined in this book, nothing stops you from breaking free from life's monotonous cycle!

At this point, I want to share a disclaimer. I know you are busy and have full lives! I acknowledge everything you are doing! To be honest, I know you may not even read this entire book! I am okay with that! What I am not okay with is you not being able to change your relationship with work because you are busy. Keep dipping into this book at your own pace! To take your exploration deeper or even if you just skim the book, I suggest doing the check-in exercises at the end of every chapter.

I invite you to join me on this exciting journey of self-discovery and growth – personal and career. Let's change the way we work!

Part I

Awareness

"Truth is the only safe ground to stand on."

–Elizabeth Cady Stanton

If you don't know what a problem is, you may never find a solution. We turn up at work every day and invest our time and effort. Yet, if we feel unfulfiled, there is a gap that we need to address. The first step towards that is to gain awareness. To uncover the truth. The truth about what is going on, what stories we tell ourselves, and how it is playing out in life.

In this section of the book, we identify tools and techniques to help us unearth this gap between where we are and where we want to be and bring to light the deeper beliefs and thoughts that cause it. Gaining clarity on our situation will not only help us understand ourselves better but also understand where we want to go from here and what we are capable of doing to make that happen.

In the following chapters, we will delve into a world of introspection and reflection. This journey can be exciting, nerve-wracking, or disturbing but will be transformational. You wouldn't be able to look at things again in the same way.

This is where our worldviews are questioned and shaped to enable us to become an Ace at Work.

Enjoy the ride!

Chapter One

Introspect

"What lies behind us and what lies before us are small matters compared to what lies within us."

–Ralph Walton Emerson

Right off the bat, let's get something straight: Advice, just because it is given freely and openly, does not mean it will work for you. Only you would know what would work for you. The real question is, do you know?

More often than not, we think we know ourselves well. We believe we know what we want, what we are good at, and what we struggle with. And indeed, nobody knows us better than ourselves. However, the fact of the matter is that what we define as ourselves includes a lot of opinions, a lot of influence, and a lot of restrictions that society, other people, upbringing, or our inner voices have set for us. It is not until we sit down and introspect that we can actually understand who we really are, what we want, and what we can do to get there. If you want to ace at work, you need to start by figuring yourself out.

Only when we know ourselves and truly understand our needs, wants, capabilities, restrictions, and challenges can we move forward in our journey where we are driven, fulfilled, and have fun in the process. So let's start with that: Introspect.

My journey with introspection didn't start until I quit my corporate job in 2020! And not a day has gone by without thinking about why I did not do this sooner! I realised that my views of the world and my relationship with work changed only when I stepped out of it! But not everyone has the luxury to leave their jobs, nor is that a requirement! If I knew then what I know now about myself, my choices in my career would be very different! I wouldn't have stayed at that toxic job. I would have known what to negotiate for. I would have not taken the other job because I got desperate. I would be more intentional in the projects I took up. I would leave work on time. And that is only the tip of the iceberg.

What does it mean to introspect? Though there are many ways you could do this, in this chapter, we will explore three options. These are the ones I have benefitted the most from. Number one is sitting in silence and giving yourself the headspace to figure things out. Number two is journaling, a means to externalise our thoughts, and number three is the power of questioning, to seek clarity. Let's dive deeper into each of these. These may sound totally unrelated to performance at work, but bear with me! As we progress in this book, it will all come together.

Sitting in Silence

Sitting in silence is a powerful way to give yourself space to truly be yourself. And when I say sit in silence, it doesn't mean sit staring into your phone. Silence. Do nothing. As simple as this sounds, it isn't.

In 2014, a team of psychologists led by Timothy Wilson at the University of Virginia conducted a study in which participants were taken through a series of experiments wherein they had to spend time alone in a room with no distractions such as books, phones, or music. In a shocking discovery (literally), in one of the experiments, it was found that 67% of men and 25% of women chose to administer a mild electric shock to themselves rather than sit alone with their thoughts.

Sitting in silence can be challenging. The key is to start small and build yourself up. Let us explore some of the ways you can start this introspection practice.

Meditation (I am sure you knew we would go there)! Meditation practices can vary from sitting and focusing on your breath or an object, or staring at the sky, to guided meditations. The intention behind it is to try and calm your mind. I remember sitting for meditation sessions and opening my eyes to feel more overwhelmed and agitated, as so many thoughts kept coming to me. Often, we are flooded with thoughts, and rightly so – our brains can't stop thinking. That's a major portion of why we have a brain in the first place! Instead of trying to stop our thoughts, we should simply let them pass and bring our attention back to the present moment. It helped me to imagine placing each thought on a leaf floating away in a stream of water.

Mindfulness practices are other tools you could explore. Doing anything you do with more focus and attention! Spending time in nature and being present in the moment by observing the sights and sounds around you is as simple as it can get. Walk barefoot and feel the grass or sand beneath your feet. You can also explore creative mediums such as mandala drawings or adult colouring books.

The purpose of sitting in silence is to start having a conversation with yourself and observe the thoughts that come to you. What kind of thoughts are these? Are they thoughts that limit you or thoughts that help you leverage your skills? Are they thoughts that make you open to opportunities, or are they negative thoughts that bring you down?

Whatever they may be, don't judge them. Simply become aware. You are who you are, not because you're helpless.

The magic of these mindful pauses in your day is that these will become pockets of insights for you. Ever had brilliant ideas in the shower or when washing dishes? I couldn't find any scientific evidence for this, but a psychological perspective of why this happens is that your mind is relaxed during those moments. Your cognitive brain, the part of the brain that processes and holds abilities associated with thinking, perceiving, learning, remembering, problem-solving, and decision-making, isn't actively in use. When your mind is at ease and not preoccupied with immediate tasks or external stimuli, it can wander more freely and make new connections.

Your subconscious plays a role in it too, where your mind continues to work on a problem or idea even when you're not consciously thinking about it!

These day-dreaming, mind-wandering moments may come in silent times, but speak volumes about us. Becoming aware of these is the first step into introspection.

Journaling

The first thoughts that came to my mind when I heard 'journaling' were the words, "Dear Diary…". In my initial days, I wrote pristine words in it and made it sound like a dreamy picture! (Hoping secretly to have a movie made of me someday :-D) I didn't start to realise the power of journaling until I stopped fabricating the words I put in it!

Journaling is a powerful tool for introspection. Our brains have thousands of thoughts each day, and we can't possibly become aware of them all. Journaling helps slow down our thinking process, record our thoughts, and make us feel lighter. When you engage in the act of writing down your thoughts, emotions, and experiences in a journal, it allows you to externalise and organise your inner world and gain a clearer perspective. I won't bore you by listing much scientific research done to identify the benefits of journaling. But I know that journaling is associated with improved mental health and works as a therapeutic tool. (Please note, it does not replace a therapist!)

This is a very personal and flexible practice, with different styles, methods, and approaches. Not every kind is needed, and not every kind will work for you. Hence, feel free to experiment and play around. It is your game, and the rules are yours to make or break! But trust in the process, that however you do it, it will add tremendous value to you.

Let's explore some of the ways of journaling.

You don't need a fancy diary with your name engraved on it. Although, it doesn't hurt to have one if it motivates you to write in it.

I am referring a lot to 'writing in a journal' as a physical act of writing on paper with a pen or pencil. However, it doesn't have to be. You could very well maintain digital journals which you can type into. While journaling by hand has its benefits of engaging multiple senses and offering a break from our constant staring-at-the-screen culture, digital journaling does come with ease of convenience and organisation. I would say it is a personal preference entirely. Don't rule out a combination of both too!

When you don't know where to start, choose a medium that suits you (hand-written or digital) and begin with brain-writing or free writing. This involves writing down whatever comes to mind on a blank page. When I started, I felt silly and unsure, but over time, it became a great way to release feelings of overwhelm and pent-up emotions.

During my first attempt at this exercise, I literally wrote, 'What the hell am I doing? I don't even know why I'm writing this.

It feels so silly.' After making fun of the process for about ten lines, I eventually reached a point where I thought, 'Well, let me give it a try.' So, I started writing about what was on my mind, like what I wanted to cook that day, and it just flowed from there. An avalanche of thoughts started flooding my mind. After doing this exercise for 10 minutes, I began to feel free, and my brain felt lighter. That's the power of journaling.

Free-flow writing has no structure, no limitations. It's like an open book where you pour yourself out onto the paper. When you write, think that this is for your eyes only. Don't try to be artistic or edit while you write. Just write with the understanding that no one else will ever read it. This nuance is really important to embrace true introspection. Don't let the "what if someone reads it!" cloud your writing.

A next level journal is more structured, and you will find many types of these journals – dotted journals, gratitude journals, reflective journals, and so on. They take on the forms of planners, including things you need to do, your calendar, and your priorities, while also providing space for gratitude, affirmations, and more.

To avoid getting overwhelmed with the options, start simple with brain-writing and planning your days. Try a few types, and you will find a sweet spot for your journal.

Personally, I am addicted to journaling now. My method is a constant work in progress, but I use a combination of structured journals and bullet journals to create my own. I have included a sample journal template along with this book, which you can find at (www.performatbest.com/books/

resources). Feel free to use it and customise it to make it your own. There is nothing like a personalised journal! You will fall in love with the work of art that is yours!

Power of Questions

Questions play a significant role. Our brains love questions. When we ask our brain a question, it naturally seeks an answer. All the millions of neurons and connections in our brain start firing up in search of that answer. Questions evoke curiosity in us and help us learn. Children are a classic example of this. Ever noticed toddlers? They ask a gazillion questions, enough to send parents and adults running for the hills or looking for cover! My son is four years old as I am writing this book, and I will exhaust the pages in it if I start listing the questions he asks. His favourite one, and mine too, is 'Why'!

Why? What? When? Where? Who? How?

There is no end to asking questions! The more questions we ask ourselves, about ourselves, the more we get out of the introspection practices. Self-reflective questions, in particular, work wonders in helping you understand yourself better. Be mindful that there are right and wrong questions to ask. If you question, "Why should I do it?" or "Why me?" then you are playing a rebel or a victim card!

To take control of your introspection and to pave the way for a path ahead, there are a few essential questions that can truly transform your practice.

- How are you feeling?
- What do you really want?
- What is the real challenge?
- Why are you doing what you're doing?
- Where are you?

These questions can be remarkable in helping you understand your current state, your desired destination, and your emotional response to various situations and track your progress. Many of your resistances, inner thoughts, and even undiscovered beliefs will start to surface on paper. Moreover, questions like "What are my values?" or "What makes me happy?" can lead to profound insights and help guide you towards a more fulfilling life.

I have compiled a list of questions you can ask yourself to initiate self-introspection. I have played it as a game and recommend it to all my coaching clients too. You can find it at www.performatbest.com/books/resources. These questions are great journaling prompts.

Some of the questions may not make sense immediately, but I encourage you to attempt them one by one. Consider tackling one question per day or whenever you engage in this introspective practice. Ask yourself a question and either sit in silence pondering about it or journal your answer. If you are up for a challenge, record yourself speaking about it.

Avoid taking on too much at once, as it can become overwhelming and have counterproductive effects. One question at a time. It can also be intense if you're not ready to accept what you actually think or feel. Set aside judgement, become aware of your conditioning, biases, and preconceived notions of right and wrong, and simply let yourself explore. Remember, this process of self-exploration and journaling can have a profound impact on your life.

If you find it challenging to do this exercise alone, you can involve a partner, such as your spouse, a friend, or a confidant. Remember that these people come with their own set of filters about life, judgements, and advice. Let's accept that nobody is perfect and try to approach this exercise as freely as possible on your own.

Engaging in discussions about these questions can be great conversation starters and will help you nurture deeper relationships with others as well. You can ask these questions to your friends or colleagues during catch-up sessions, and you may find yourself having deep conversations. Prepare to be surprised in getting to know people in a whole new light.

It helps when you and another person are both on the same journey and then you can hold each other accountable and share conversations by answering the questions together.

If you find it challenging to be open and honest in these discussions with the people around you, I highly recommend taking these discussions up with a professional coach. A coach sets the grounds for a safe space and holds no judgements.

Any thoughts I am unable to process myself, a coach always helps me through them!

Introspection At Work

I did mention earlier that advice may not work for everyone, but it's important to become aware of why it does not work for you and whether that reason is real or if it's something your mind is creating out of fear. We all have different perceptions of the world around us, and introspection brings light to our unconscious biases and helps us understand ourselves better.

As we progress through this book, I want you to start becoming aware of your thoughts and introspecting on where they are coming from and what is triggering them. Pay attention to what conversations you are having with yourself or what thoughts are getting triggered by the ideas presented in this book. Whether you agree or disagree with an idea, introspect on why you feel the way you do about it. This awareness is what will give you the insights you need to move forward.

Throughout this book, I will be sharing different concepts and ideas, and guiding you through various activities and challenges. As you explore these, there will be a part of you that either agrees or disagrees with what is being written. To take introspection seriously, ask yourself where these reactions are coming from and start paying attention to the conversations you have with yourself. Be curious about the thoughts and emotions that arise in response to the ideas presented.

If, for example, I suggest leaving work on time, observe your immediate reaction. You might find yourself saying, "Absolutely, I agree, and I already do that," or you might respond with, "That's not possible for me. My office is too chaotic, and my boss expects me to stay late." Whatever thoughts arise, become aware of them. This awareness is crucial because it provides you with the necessary insight to move forward.

Embrace introspection as an ongoing practice. Dedicate time to sit in silence, journal your thoughts and experiences, and ask yourself powerful questions. Be open to uncovering new insights, challenging your assumptions, and growing personally and professionally.

As you delve deeper into the pages of this book, allow introspection to guide you on a profound journey of self-discovery. The path may not always be easy, but the rewards are immeasurable—a life lived with intention, authenticity, and fulfilment.

Let's embark on this introspective adventure together and unlock the tremendous potential that lies within you. Get ready to transform your life and achieve your highest aspirations.

The journey starts now.

Chapter Summary

By taking the time to truly understand ourselves and our needs, we can shift our perspective from fear and stress to meaning and fulfilment. As you engage in introspection, you'll begin to understand yourself better, unravel the layers of societal influences, and discover your authentic desires and aspirations.

Overall, the key takeaways from the chapter are:

- Sitting in silence helps create self-awareness and can lead to insights and new connections. Sitting in silence involves creating space for oneself without distractions and observing the thoughts that arise.
- Journaling allows individuals to externalise thoughts, emotions, and experiences, leading to improved mental health.
- Questioning stimulates curiosity and self-reflection, helping individuals gain insights and understand themselves better.
- Asking self-reflective questions such as "How are you feeling?" and "What do you really want?" helps gain insights into one's current state and desired goals.

Embrace the power of introspection, and you will pave the way for a more driven, fulfilled, and enjoyable life, and not just ace at work.

In the further chapters, we will explore how we can take introspection further and use it as fuel to dive deeper into understanding ourselves and our relationships with work.

Check-In Exercise

At this point in the book, take a moment to check-in with what you take away from this chapter.

- *What about introspection catches your attention?*
- *How do you rate your introspection skills on a scale of 1 to 10 (10 being the highest)?*
- *What will you do to increase your score by 1?*

Try the following:

- *Determine which introspection technique you will explore.*
- *When and how will you do it?*
- *Grab your journal prompts and templates from www.performatbest.com/books/resources.*

Chapter Two

Get Real

"The truth is rarely pure and never simple."

–Oscar Wilde

At the risk of being hated or causing you to stop reading this book, I will share with you three harsh truths we all need to be aware of.

Number One: You are not doing anyone a favour by doing your job; you simply get paid for it. You are selling your time and effort for money, which comes to you every month in the form of your salary. So stop acting like the world owes you a job or that everybody in your team needs to tolerate you because you are turning up. There is no obligation for them to do anything for you. However, you need that job to make money or fulfil any dependencies you have on it, or simply because you enjoy it. So, get real and ask yourself why you are in that job.

Number Two: You are not entitled. This is not like school where you progress from one grade to another every year.

You cannot be guaranteed or promised promotions every year or every few years. Your career growth is not inherently tied to your job. Every career path is unique, and you need to work on it intentionally. The more intentional you are, the more it will help you grow in the way you want. So, you can't just go about doing your work and expect to be automatically promoted because you've been in the company for a certain number of years. That's not how it works. You could be stuck in one position for 10 years without getting a promotion, or you could be getting promotions every few months. It depends entirely on the nature of the company, the industry, the environment, and many other factors that are beyond our control. Be aware and get real with yourself that simply doing your work, following instructions, and keeping your head down does not guarantee a promotion or even a raise.

Number Three: You are a cog in a machine and easily replaceable. You are hired to fill a need or gap in the company for a simple reason: your skill set matches that need. There are many other people (and even machines, nowadays) that can do your job. If you are not bringing anything unique to the table that nobody else can do, then you should be worried that your position is at risk during layoffs or cost-cutting measures in the company. If you feel your company values you and loves you and you would not be in that position, then you better have a damn convincing explanation. The moment things get tough in a company, all that love is tested!

I understand that these truths might make you angry, or something stirred in you and triggered some thoughts. I want you to acknowledge that feeling and listen to your internal dialogue. What is your voice telling you right now? Are you saying, "This is not me. None of this will happen to me," and justifying your behaviour? Or are you telling yourself, "Yes, I am not in this situation because I have done so much work, and I'm known for it! I'm growing, and I'm in a great place in my job"? The chances are you belong to the former category and aspire to become someone who belongs to the latter. Take a moment to think about it and consider whether I'm challenging your assumptions or helping you rethink your job.

What You Really Do

Let's dive deeper into what you really do at your job. I'm willing to bet that most of your time goes into what I call the big three: checking emails, attending meetings, and firefighting. These tasks may seem like work, but they aren't necessarily what you should be prioritising. You weren't hired for your position just to reply to emails or attend meetings. You were hired to contribute your expertise and help the company thrive. Are you truly doing that? Or is most of your time spent on meaningless and pointless tasks? It's essential to evaluate whether these tasks align with the company's objectives. While it may feel like certain emails or meetings are crucial for the progress of projects, and that could very well be the case, you need to ask yourself if your primary needle-moving tasks revolve around them. Awareness is key.

To become more aware, start auditing your work. Look at it from a distance, separating your emotions and personal attachments. List down everything you do in a day at work. Make note of each task and, if possible, the time it takes to do it. And I mean EVERY TASK - be it replying to emails, picking up a phone call, taking a coffee break, or being distracted by social media! Whatever it is, be honest with yourself and write it down - without any filtering, without any judgements. If you are immediately going, "I don't have time for this!", then I 1000% encourage you to do it! Because clearly, your time isn't really helping you! Do this for even a couple of days and review it. What you essentially get is an objective view of reality! Analyse how much of your time is spent on what kind of tasks. This may be uncomfortable for you, and I get it! I have been there too! I saw my task list and said to myself, "Yikes! Who will promote me for doing THAT?!"

The way we see our world is our view! There is more to the world when we see it from the eyes of others! (I may have started to sound a bit philosophical here! Bear with me!) Once you have your view of what you do at work, it is time to check-in with others. Who specifically? Your Boss! Whether you realise it or not, this already happens to a certain extent in the form of appraisal meetings. Have you ever walked into an appraisal meeting feeling confident of doing a good job, felt that you have done everything you possibly could, and had your bubble burst when your manager says, "You have been average"? I know, it sucks! Feels like you wasted an entire year! I hate that feeling and can take a chance that you do too. I can bet you started to resent your manager, hate your team, or blame the company! I have been guilty of saying, 'Okay, this company is like that. It's a difficult time.' We come up with a million excuses to justify what happened so we can feel better in the moment! All this is an indication that you may not be transparent with yourself. Get Real!

Matters of the Boss and Folks

Have a more functioning relationship with your boss and have frequent catch-up sessions. Make these work for you! Use these discussions to not only give a status update but to gather feedback on your work and understand what are the big, pressing challenges for the team and the company! Also, start paying attention to what your boss is working on. What things are getting discussed in the management meetings? What issues are getting escalated and gaining pressure? What are the things that make the management team say, "Drop everything you are doing and work on this"? These various observations point to things that really matter and are their priorities. How much of your task list is aligned toward working on these?

Another source of information is the water cooler gossip! When colleagues hang around and chat or gossip! What are people saying about you? What are the things people come to you for? This will give you tremendous feedback on what it is other people see you do! Is this aligned with what you are actually good at and want to be known for? Or are you just working on distractions?

If you start to see gaps between what you think you do, and how other people see it, you have a starting point to change your relationship with work.

Look at your identified task list and honestly determine how much of your tasks are helping you move towards your goals and are aligned with your strengths and ambitions! If you don't have goals or are unsure about how to identify the value-adding tasks, that is a topic of discussion we will get to in the further chapters.

While reviewing your list, you are bound to face some questions. What am I doing wrong? What should I be doing if not this? Many times, we find ourselves questioning "What am I doing with my life?". Well, if that's you, I can totally understand where you're coming from. We often find ourselves doing work we may not necessarily enjoy, or work that does not make us come alive or feel fulfilled. And yet we pour in our heart and soul in it and we expect to get rewarded for our efforts. And none of this is wrong. It is a combination of our actions, beliefs, and circumstances. We find ourselves in situations where we feel like work has been unfair to us. It isn't giving us the necessary recognition. We feel underappreciated, unrecognised, and it feels like we are working non-stop, and work sucks up life. Now, if that's you, I want you to take a moment now and apply all of your introspection techniques to get real with yourself. Hit pause, and ponder on the question, are you really performing or are you hiding in the system?

Hiding In The System

What does this even mean? Being a top performer means going beyond expectations, taking ownership of your work, and actively seeking opportunities to contribute and make a difference. On the other hand, hiding in the system means just doing what is asked of you without intentionally putting in any extra effort or taking initiative. If they are told to send an email, they will send an email and nothing more. They won't follow-up or complete a task unless the manager checks up on them. You might meet the minimum requirements, but you won't stand out as an exceptional employee.

I am sure you have seen these people who are 'hiding in the system' at your workplace. They are not the ones first up for any promotion, nor are they at the bottom of the barrel, per se.

Don't recognise anyone? Here's one clue: They cc their boss on every email! They sneeze, and the boss is updated about it! This is, in my world, fake work! Showcasing something that isn't concrete or highlighting every small thing done! I feel people resort to such measures for two reasons. Number 1, they don't have significant work to showcase. Number 2, they are insecure about their job. If you were a top performer, you wouldn't need to loop in your boss on every little thing. The big results will speak for themselves!

Another characteristic of the ones 'hiding in the system' is creating a false sense of ownership. These people hoard information and are secretive or selective about sharing or teaching others. They feel an ego boost when people come to them for something. Being transparent, open, and willing to help are not necessarily their keywords of choice. I could never wrap my head around colleagues like this – sharing half-baked information, not training anyone else to do their job, and communicating only on a need-to-know basis! They seem to come across as just bad team players! Don't get me wrong, sometimes you can be an independent contributor who owns things end to end and doesn't really work with others. I get it! These are great executors! But in reality, they work in silos. Nobody really understands what or how they work, and this also limits their possibilities of expanding their work. They can't even take a decent vacation because nobody else can do what they do!

A 'hider' can also be spotted if they are the first to arrive and the last to leave! Office timings don't seem to be a thing for them to pay attention to! When you finish your work, leave! I remember one of my colleagues would loiter around the office, sit replying to emails, or spend time on his phone and do whatever to look busy – until our manager left, and then he would scram for the door. God forbid he ever left the office a minute before my manager! Working late is a pandemic in its own right! You don't get fired or noticed for leaving work on time! As long as your work is done, you are delivering to expectations; nobody expects you to stay late! It is all in our minds! Try asking your manager once, "I finished my work, can I leave on time?" and see if he fires you! On a lighter note, he may give you more work! (But you don't have to do it right then unless explicitly specified!). An extreme of this is being online or sending emails at ungodly hours! Ever received an email at 2 am in the morning? I wouldn't blame the person sending it, but I would blame you if you checked it at 2 am while working in a 9 to 5-ish job! Busy times, peak hours, international clients – all can be forms of excuses! Get real! Are you working late because you weren't efficient in finishing work on time, or is this a temporary workload, or that's just how my work is? Are you hiding in the system?

In being honest and doing your bit of introspection, what you are essentially doing is clarifying if this is a 'you' problem or if it really is a workplace challenge! Even if it is the latter, there are ways around it! I hope to give you numerous strategies to work efficiently and effectively in this book, whereby you would be working fewer hours and delivering more quality work! Sounds good, doesn't it?

It's time to break free from complacency and adopt a proactive and growth-oriented mindset about work. Embrace the challenge of becoming a top performer who consistently delivers exceptional results and actively contributes to the success of your team and organisation, thereby crafting your own career trajectory.

Remember, the choice is yours. You have the power to reshape your approach to work and create a fulfilling and impactful career.

Chapter Summary

Many of us find ourselves questioning our purpose at work and feeling unfulfiled. We may pour our heart and soul into our jobs but feel underappreciated and stuck. It's crucial to be honest with ourselves, reflect on our own doings, and take ownership of our growth.

Overall, the key takeaways from the chapter are:

- Understand that you aren't entitled and are replaceable in the workforce, so focus on delivering unique value and constantly improving.
- Audit your work to identify tasks that truly contribute to the company's objectives and prioritise them.
- Seek feedback from your boss, colleagues, and performance appraisals to gain awareness of how your work is perceived.
- Align your perception of your work with how others perceive it to bridge any gaps and improve effectiveness.
- Avoid hiding in the system by merely doing the bare minimum; strive to be a top performer in your team.
- Practise open and transparent communication, sharing necessary information to foster trust and collaboration.
- Avoid working in isolation; establish connections and collaborate with others to enhance your growth opportunities.

These takeaways aim to help you reassess your approach to work, gain awareness of your performance, and take proactive steps toward career growth and transformation.

A big piece of the puzzle is to clarify to yourself what you really do and align it as much as possible with what 'makes you come alive' and feel fulfilled at work. That is the nuance we will discuss next.

Check-In Exercise

At this point in the book, take a moment to check-in with what you take away from this chapter.

- *How do you really feel about your work?*
- *How do you rate your fulfilment level at work on a scale of 1 to 10 (10 being the highest)?*
- *What will you do to increase your score by 1?*

Try the following:

1. *Make a list of everything you do at work.*
2. *Analyse the data after a couple of days/week to find patterns and behaviours.*
3. *Identify what tasks are making you cringe and what excites you.*

Chapter Three

Lay The Table

> *"Passion is energy. Feel the power that comes from focusing on what excites you."*
>
> *–Oprah Winfrey*

With all the introspection that we have been doing, there is a high tendency for us to get into our heads. We are thinking a lot about things, and sometimes even overthinking them. We are, after all, human! This activity might range from being empowering or sending us on a downward spiral that ends with "I am no good". Whatever happens to you, know that you are not alone. We are in our heads!

It's time to get out of your head and gain massive clarity. It's time to answer the big question: "What do you bring to the table?"

This is a typical interview question that you are asked to understand your fitment for a position. Interviewers are specifically looking for your capabilities, skills, and strengths that align with the requirements of the role they are trying to fill. Hence, this bit of awareness is driven by knowing what truly makes you effective or ineffective in your job. This introspection is crucial because it helps you define for yourself the value you bring to that particular role and understand why you are irreplaceable. As we have briefly discussed in the previous chapter, you are replaceable! You are replaceable if you merely focus on a set of skills without incorporating your unique elements or additional skill set. In such a case, anyone else could easily take your place. For instance, if you excel at Java coding, you can be substituted by another skilled Java coder. I don't mean to offend you by saying you are not skilled enough, but it is a reality. It is never just about the tasks you perform at work; there's much more happening behind the scenes.

Whatever the environment you are working in or the work that you do, the one variable that is in your understanding (and control) is YOU! When you turn up at work (even if you dragged your feet to it), you don't just come to do your work. You bring along with you your life experiences, beliefs, and values. However, not all of these beliefs are empowering; many of them can be limiting. They may not necessarily add value to our work or lives and hinder our personal growth.

The purpose of this book is to shed light on these non-empowering limiting beliefs and question them. When you come to work, you bring along your strengths, weaknesses, skills, competencies, wants, needs, and emotions. You are more than you think. You bring more to your work every day than what you believe or consciously acknowledge. How do we become aware of these? How do we truly understand our capabilities? We start by introspecting! (Of course, by now you know the drill). By asking yourself questions and utilising the various tools we have discussed so far, you will gain clarity and understand what you bring to the table.

An add-on to this is using self-assessment tools. From discovering personality types to identifying strengths and blockers, there are numerous tools available for free or a small fee. Sometimes, these tools can even shift your understanding because our perception of ourselves may differ from the results of these assessments. We will discuss more about these in this chapter. But please proceed with a disclaimer. It is important to acknowledge that these assessment tools may have limitations in terms of their accuracy. And also, just because certain things are identified about you in the assessments, it doesn't define you or limit you. There is no single comprehensive assessment that can be 100% accurate, simply because we are all such complex beings. If you don't like something, you can always work on changing it. There is no right or wrong! They are just parameters about you and make you who you are. Embrace them with an open mind.

These tools and your introspections can help you identify answers to the looming question of what you bring to the table – strengths, weaknesses, skills, and competencies! Let's look at each of these aspects individually.

Strengths

First, let's talk about strengths. Strengths are things that come easily to you, things that you can rely on, and things that you are good at. It's like a matter of instinct or inherent ability. These are things that you can do easily, but you often see some other people struggling to do or understand.

Identifying your strengths can be challenging for many people because they may not fully understand or recognise them. We are flooded with thoughts along the lines of, "Yeah, I am good at this, but I wouldn't call it my strength", "There are people better than me in it", or the worst, "I am not really good at anything". I belonged to this category.

To begin, I challenge you to start making a list of things that you are really good at. You are more of an expert than you realise. I can almost guarantee that after writing a few things down, you will exhaust that list and struggle to come up with anything else. There are many things that people tend to underestimate about themselves. There are often many strengths that we overlook or fail to identify within ourselves. I exhausted my list when I filled in 12 things! Doing this exercise frequently, I am able to grow that list to over 50 things I am good at!

Here is where you dig deeper, and when you eventually run out of things to list as your strengths, look around. Consider the things that others seek your assistance with. Observe the activities, tasks, or subject matters for which people approach you. As an alternative to this, you can reach out to the people who know you well and ask, "What do you think I am good at?". This exercise was nerve-wracking for me, and I can understand if it is for you too. I dreaded asking people this question. I made strides by asking my family first, then a couple of close friends.

We are often held back by our fears of being judged to even dare try it out. But trust me when I say this, this exercise is eye-opening (not just for you but for those you ask)! You will be pleasantly surprised by the things people observe about you. A friend of mine told me he thought I was great at simplifying concepts, a skill I never acknowledged I had.

You are asking for some positive feedback, and it will only make you feel better. And since giving praise and noticing good things in people isn't a natural thing for many people, when someone is asked to do this, they are changing their perspectives about you too. You can share positive things about the other person first to ease them into the exercise. For valuable insights, remember to ask your close friends, family, and co-workers and not people you had only a few interactions with. People's perspectives may differ from your own. Take it in your stride and learn about how you come across. I believe I am a kind of perfectionist but draw the line at 'good enough'. But a friend told me she thought I was carefree!

This list that you are building can help you identify areas that are your strengths and where you are considered an expert. Let's delve into the concept of being an expert. Many individuals, including myself and my clients, often struggle with this term. We often feel that we are not experts in anything. Here's something I heard that has impacted me heavily. I used to struggle to call myself an 'expert' at anything. I am good at things, but I am no expert! I thought long years of experience, higher degrees on a subject topic, or large followings on social media were parameters of an 'expert'. A mentor of mine did a little exercise, which I think you should do too! Rate yourself on a scale of 1 to 10 (10 being highest) on how strong you are in a particular aspect. For instance, you scored a six on communication skills. You, my dear friend, are an expert communicator for anyone who scored a 1 to 5! So, give yourself more credit than you usually do because you are an expert in some area or another for someone. Determine what that area is.

While making your list, pay attention to that inner voice that arises. Sometimes, when you write down a few things that you feel okay about, that voice becomes louder and starts telling you, "You are right! You are the best at it". It may also bring up doubts by suggesting that you were lucky, or some external factor was responsible. We may end up not recognising our abilities. Even with evidence of our accomplishments, we feel like a fraud or feel inadequate. This is commonly known as imposter syndrome. Give yourself some leeway, acknowledge your strengths, and take ownership of them. Believe in yourself! That is what confidence is all about!

Weaknesses

Weaknesses are essentially things that are difficult, challenging, or stressful for you to do. Weaknesses can be pretty obvious when you start procrastinating to do it or never 'feel' like doing it.

Here I wouldn't recommend creating a list of weaknesses because we tend to be very negative toward ourselves. If you were to make such a list, it would likely be long and potentially detrimental to your self-esteem. But if you really want to try this exercise, I suggest writing the list and then destroying it later. You can burn it, tear it apart, or engage in some other form of symbolic action to let go of those negative emotions associated with your weaknesses. This can be a powerful way to overcome these mind blocks, build confidence, and address low self-esteem.

Remember, reading the list and destroying it serves as a reminder that these weaknesses do not define you. It is a way to challenge and overcome the negative influence they may have on your self-perception.

Asking people isn't also very wise unless you take a few preparatory steps. When asking people for help in identifying your weaknesses or negative sides, prepare mentally to be bombarded. Don't get defensive or judgemental about the other person. They may not know the right way to share such feedback! We will discuss more about asking and giving feedback in further chapters of this book.

Weaknesses are only a part of who you are, and they can all be improved upon if you have the desire to develop your skills.

But more often than not, a lot of things we consider weaknesses can be driven by deeply held beliefs. These weaknesses can be brought to light by asking yourself the question, "What is stopping you from doing a certain thing?". They can manifest in various forms, and when you ask yourself this question, it reveals answers that may include self-doubt, a lack of certain skills, or a failure to appreciate what we have.

While it is debatable whether you should really focus on your weaknesses, I am of the opinion that one should focus on strengths but has to work on their weaknesses if you want to fuel your growth. After all, a chain is as strong as its weakest link. Your weaknesses should be brought to light but should not limit you. Identifying our weaknesses helps us navigate toward work that doesn't fill us with regret and stress. This awareness isn't about becoming better at your weakness, but knowing and acknowledging it so you can deal with related tasks tactfully. You don't have to do them, but you will know better to ask for help or delegate such tasks.

Skills & Competencies

Skills are essentially your ability to perform certain tasks, and they are developed through your experiences in both work and life. Skills can be broadly classified into different categories. In the context of the workplace, we typically refer to a combination of technical and personal skills.

Personal skills are qualities such as leadership, teamwork, problem-solving, communication, planning and organising, creativity, and more. On the other hand, technical skills can be categorised into two types: basic skills and specialised skills.

Basic skills include fundamental abilities like computing, typing, reading, driving, and working with numbers. Specialised skills, on the other hand, pertain to operating specific systems, utilising particular software, programming, or possessing in-depth knowledge within your specific field of work.

You may have been hired for a position based on your skill set that aligns with the job requirements. However, it is not until we start working that we realise that there are certain additional skill sets required to perform that job well. For instance, I got hired for a job based on my skill set of software-specific knowledge and qualifications, but in reality, I needed a lot of sales skills. This not being my forte made it difficult for me to perform my job. I did ok, but it was stressful! I needed to learn, adapt, and continuously grow. What I am trying to say is that we need to become aware of the first-level skills for a job and hidden skills too. You can't blame the HR or a hiring manager for not making it clear to you at the beginning as they may also not be fully aware. We have to start developing this habit of reading between the lines. These are what uncover what are known as skill gaps. These skill gaps occur when there is a mismatch between the skills required for a certain role and the skills you currently possess. Identifying these gaps provides clarity on the skills you need to acquire or improve to excel in that role.

Assess your skills! Rate your abilities on a rating scale, have discussions around your performance appraisals, or engage in online assessments and quizzes to evaluate yourself.

Much like strengths and weaknesses, the idea is to identify the gaps and be mindful and actionable about filling them, and don't judge yourself. There are enough people around us to do that for us.

While skills are specific abilities that you can learn and develop, competencies are broader sets of attributes that encompass skills, knowledge, behaviours, and attitudes. Competency refers to the ability to successfully or efficiently perform a task. Competencies take into account not only what you can do (skills) but also how you approach tasks and interact with others in a given context.

Skills and competencies, like anything else, are muscles that can be built, learned, and developed. No one is born with all the needed skills. It is just that some individuals have dedicated more attention to getting better at their skills. Create an action plan based on what you have identified, and work on equipping yourself with needed skills through books, courses, training, or hands-on experiences. You decide what you need to improve on and then improve on it!

Wants & Needs

This is probably the most important and fulfilling reflection that you will be doing – understanding your wants and needs. But first, let us understand what we mean by them. Wants are desires to possess or achieve something. In the context of the workplace, wants may include aspirations for a promotion, a salary raise, or an interest in working on specific projects or requirements. On the other hand, needs are essential or important requirements, often a necessity for survival. Let us understand the difference with some examples.

You may want a higher salary or additional financial perks like bonuses or stock options to feel valued and motivated. You need a salary that is fair and competitive for your role and responsibilities to meet your basic living expenses and financial security.

You may want more flexible working hours or the option to work remotely to achieve a better work-life balance and have more control over your schedules. You need a reasonable work-life balance to prevent burnout, maintain well-being, and sustain long-term productivity.

You may want opportunities for career advancement and promotions to fulfil your ambitions and achieve higher positions within the organisation. You need access to training, skill development, and growth opportunities to enhance your job performance and remain relevant in a dynamic work environment.

You may want a modern and aesthetically pleasing workspace with amenities like recreational areas, on-site cafes, or wellness facilities for a more enjoyable work environment. You need a safe, comfortable, and well-equipped workspace that supports your productivity and overall well-being.

You may want long-term job security and stability to alleviate concerns about layoffs or company restructuring. You need clear communication and transparency from management about the organisation's stability and future plans to feel secure in their roles.

I want to bring your attention to some wording in these examples. When referring to wants, I use the term 'may want' deliberately to acknowledge that not everyone wants the same things. However, there is no 'may' when referring to needs, because these are absolute essentials. Still, the needs may differ from person to person.

Understanding the distinction between wants and needs allows us to prioritise what we truly require from our jobs. Understanding what YOU want and need from a job changes everything! To gain clarity on these matters, you can reflect on introspective questions such as: What do you want in your job? What do you need to make it happen? And what do you require from the job to find fulfilment?

By considering these aspects and answering these introspective questions, you can better understand your wants, needs, and aspirations within your job and identify the steps necessary for personal and professional growth in your specific role.

Answering these questions will provide you with a clearer understanding of the distinction between YOUR wants and needs. These are not templates that you can apply to your life. These are entirely subjective to you! It will help you articulate your inner understanding. Although the answers to these questions can run from simple statements to pages, it is important to clarify your top wants and needs from the work you do.

Achieve crystal-clear clarity regarding your wants because if a particular role or job does not fulfil your needs or provide a direction to pursue your wants, it doesn't make sense to exhaust yourself for a job that won't contribute to your growth. Burning the midnight oil for such a job will only lead to burnout. You can save yourself years of turmoil and 'hoping' things get better.

Becoming aware of these aspects also empowers you to have more fruitful negotiations at work and during appraisals. You will discover what your red flags are and where you can be flexible.

Tools At Your Disposal

Lay out all the information on the table and create a comprehensive list, or multiple lists. Identify your strengths, weaknesses, skills, competencies, wants, and needs. Look for any skill gaps that you can fill or areas in which you can learn, develop, and build new skills.

Most importantly, these exercises and introspection help you understand your own value. Once you recognise your worth, you will begin to take ownership of yourself, give yourself credit, and work towards safeguarding your own peace of mind. When these elements are in place, you will realise that your career is in your hands. You can take small or big steps and start designing plans to create a career path that aligns with your passions, brings fulfilment, and adds meaning to your life.

We have explored here ways of self-reflection and discussions to gain this awareness. I want to take a moment here to equip you with additional methods of identifying your strengths and weaknesses too. I am listing here some of my favourite finds and is by no means the best or exhaustive list of everything that is available! Some of these are free and some are paid, and I am not gaining any benefits for promoting these tools. I am sharing these as I have taken these tests myself and have found them incredibly useful in increasing my awareness.

1. Clifton Strengths Assessment by Gallup

   This tool indicates what makes you unique across different categories. The report indicates your top strengths and weaknesses and gives you in-depth insights into tips for utilising your strengths and how to navigate your weaknesses. I found it worth my buck!

2. VIA Character Strengths Survey

   This tool helps identify positive character traits in us, and the degree to which we possess different character strengths. It is very useful to understand ourselves and how we play out in life and at work. It boosted my understanding of myself and validated a few things I was aware of.

3. Myers-Briggs Type Indicator Tests

   Various versions of this test exist. The test helps you determine which of the 16 personality types describes you best. When you discover your own personality type, you'll understand more clearly why you do the things you do.

You will gain confidence in your strengths and be better able to make decisions that suit your true nature.

Chapter Summary

Knowing what you bring to the table is about clarifying to yourself your strengths, weaknesses, skills, competencies, wants, and needs. This plays a crucial role in recognising your own value and taking ownership of your career.

Key takeaways from this chapter are:

- Introspection is crucial to understand yourself better and discover what you bring to the table.
- Seek feedback from others to gain insights into your strengths and skills that you may not be aware of.
- Recognise and embrace your strengths, as they are the qualities that come naturally to you and set you apart.
- Identify and acknowledge your weaknesses, but don't let them define you.
- Work on improving and developing skills through learning and practice.
- Understand the distinction between wants and needs in your job. Prioritise fulfilling your needs while aligning your wants to find job satisfaction.

Continuous self-assessment and improvement are vital. Knowing yourself, identifying areas of improvement, filling skill gaps, exploring new opportunities, and adapting to changes in the professional landscape are an endless journey. Make it worth your effort and time.

With awareness in place, it is now time to move forward in identifying areas of change and improvement to drive us on our career growth and fulfilment. Read on to apply this newfound awareness about yourself in the workplace and get noticed for being an ace performer.

Check-In Exercise

At this point in the book, take a moment to check-in with what you take away from this chapter.

- *What do you bring to the table?*
- *How do you rate your self-awareness levels on a scale of 1 to 10 (10 being the highest)?*
- *What will you do to increase your score by 1?*

Try the following:

- *Make a list of your strengths.*
- *Identify gaps between where you are and where you want to be.*
- *Identify skills to develop to bridge the gap and plan how you will build them.*

Part II

Change

"If we were meant to stay in one place, we'd have roots instead of feet."

–Rachel Wolchin

Knowing is one thing, but doing something about it is another. This section of the book delves into the aspect of what you can do to close the 'gap' between where we are and where we want to be. There are many things that you could do and endless ideas! Here, we will explore some of the most significant changes that you can start with.

Change can be scary. The uncertainty, the doubt, and the fear are all valid. But they shouldn't stop us from changing, nevertheless. In the following chapters, we will discover small changes to our mindsets and work habits to help us make our work easier. These nuances of approaching our work differently help us fuel our career growth and fulfilment.

You cannot continue to do what you do and expect things to drastically change. I urge you to be open-minded and approach these ideas with the reflective approach discovered in the previous sections. As simple as they sound, the ideas will have a profound impact on the way you approach work. Becoming an Ace at Work begins here!

Chapter Four

Be Proactive

"The capacity to learn is a gift, the ability to learn is a skill, the willingness to learn is a choice."

–Brian Herbert

If you don't ask, the answer is always no. This line has made me think very deeply about the way we work, function, and think. It indeed is true. I heard from a friend that she often missed out on her promotions. When she was talking to other people in her company and finding out why she was actually not getting promoted, she realised that most people who did get promoted asked for it. They made their intentions very clear upfront, saying that they wanted to get promoted this year and worked in alignment with that. And it's not just about promotions; whenever you need any kind of help, feedback, or input from somebody, you will never get it unless you ask for it. Asking isn't about waiting for others to come to you so you can ask; it's about being proactive. If you don't put yourself out there and take that first step or initiative to reach out to people for their input, you will be left hanging, and you will keep feeling stuck or helpless.

Being proactive is taking things into your control and not just reacting to everything life throws at you. It just means putting yourself first in the right way. Because only when you establish healthy boundaries for your work and mental space will you be able to perform to the best of your abilities. Being proactive means putting yourself first and taking that initial initiative because you want to have control over how the discussions, conversations, or outcomes unfold. It's about understanding yourself, understanding your needs, and prioritising them. Being proactive is about asking, setting intentions, and finding opportunities. Let us explore these further.

Ask And You Shall Seek

Taking the first step to approach someone for something is often necessary in practice. As we discussed at the start of this chapter, it can also become crucial and necessary too. You need to ask before you can receive it! But, but, but… I am sure many questions flood our brains right now – what to ask for, whom to ask, how to ask? Hold your horses! I won't leave you hanging with these questions.

Ask for advice (from the right people), input for your work, help with something, and most importantly – feedback! A tiny nuance to this – ask wisely! Although I am a believer in 'there is no such thing as a stupid question', I do believe that some due diligence can be applied at our end before we ask.

For example, if Google can answer some simple questions, especially knowledge-based ones, then Google is who you ask! Not your boss! What I am trying to say is, it is ok to ask even a question that may seem silly, but don't make it your mission to ask silly questions or not give it a thought before asking.

The important thing to address is the underlying thoughts and beliefs. A lot of the time, we don't ask for help as we fear judgement or rejection. What if they don't agree?! What will they think about me?! We start building stories in our head that others will think I am incapable or weak if I ask. She doesn't know this much also?! But in reality, asking will only benefit you! Try to recall situations where asking for some help has actually helped you!

Now, how do you approach somebody for it? It's a simple three-step process: 1) Build a relationship, 2) Have clarity, and 3) Be understanding. Let's look at these in detail.

First, building a relationship. Asking things from known people like friends, family, and colleagues is fairly easier than asking total strangers. There is some comfort there, as there is a relationship already established. I don't discourage you from reaching out to strangers. It doesn't mean that you can walk up to a stranger and ask, "Hey, can you give me some feedback?" You may receive vague answers or no appropriate response at all. That wouldn't necessarily be helpful. It is only when we have a level of trust or a certain relationship with someone that we can openly and confidently reach out to them and ask for what we want and get a useful response. It's not about becoming best friends with everybody but having a functional working relationship where you understand the dynamics of that relationship.

Second, when you don't know what you're asking for, you may receive things you never asked for. It's important to be clear about what you want at any given point in time, what you expect from others, or what you want to accomplish. Let's take an example to better understand this. If you approach a colleague after a presentation and ask, "Hey, can you tell me how the presentation went?" There's a high chance they will just say, "Hey, that was a good attempt. It was great," or provide vague answers. However, if you ask, "Can you tell me how the slides of my presentation were? Did you like the way it was put together?" Their feedback would be more specific to the slides and their content. That feedback is more useful for you to implement in future presentations. Similarly, if you ask someone to recommend a book without specifying your preferences, they may suggest random books or authors. But if you are clear about asking for a light, easy-to-read book to get started with reading, their recommendations would be different. Be as clear as possible on what you are asking.

Third, be understanding. When we ask for help, the other person may not be in a position to assist us right away or at all. This is when some of us start to feel anxious or frustrated, thinking, "I asked for help, and they didn't do it." We tend to take things personally or judge the other person. When somebody says no to you, the first thing to understand is that it's not about you. It doesn't mean they don't like you, don't want to help you, or that there's an issue with your relationship. It could simply mean something entirely different. For example, they might be busy, swamped with other tasks, or have different priorities. The particular thing you're asking for may not be at the top of their list, so they say no. In fact, I respect people who say no because they understand boundaries and value your time and relationship. It's better than saying yes and struggling with it themselves or delivering subpar outcomes.

Being more understanding allows us to view things differently. Maybe the person is busy or not the right person to help, or perhaps it was the wrong time or place when we asked. Keeping these factors in mind, it's crucial for us to understand that when we approach someone for something, we need to be open to how the conversation will flow and how the outcomes will be defined.

It helps to think about the worst-case scenario before asking someone. If you have this question in mind, you'll realise that the worst thing that can happen is they say no, which wouldn't have any significant effects. However, we often fear that if we ask, they will think we are weak or inexperienced. These thoughts are usually driven by fear - fear of judgement or losing respect or the relationship we're reaching out to. More often than not, that is never the case.

Intentions

Even before you ask, you first need to know what to ask for! Here is where intentions come into place. Intentions can be in the form of clarifying your wants or setting goals. If you don't set goals, someone else will set them for you. If you don't set your own goals and don't clarify why you're doing what you're doing and what outcome you expect to achieve, your manager, boss, or somebody else in your company will set them for you. And here's the thing – It is OK! The question to ask here is this – is it ok with you? I totally understand that sometimes the goals need to come from the higher-ups so that we are aligned with the bigger objectives and goals of the company. But in that case, don't complain about your life not being under your control. It's obvious that if you're not driving your car, somebody else is, and it's okay to accept that. (We, of course, love chauffeur-driven rides). But you need to have an idea of where the driver is taking you, and if it is not where you like going, then you have some other wants. The first section of this book has taken you through various approaches to clarify this for yourself. If the goals set for you don't seem okay, and if it's not something you want to do, then start taking things into your own hands and set your goals. Have discussions with your peers, team members, managers, or people around you at work to ensure that your work is aligned with your personal objectives and not just with the company's objectives.

If this sounds selfish, pause right here. I highly recommend reflecting on what part of this is sounding selfish! If you, doing work you enjoy and feel aligned with is selfish, then you better be! It is your life! You drive it! The sooner you wrap your head around this, the better it is!

Be intentional about what you want and know to ask for it. It's common for us to ask for help and hope that things will be done as expected or that we will achieve the desired outcome.

However, it's important to recognise that hope alone is not a strategy. You can hope and pray for things to go your way, or you can be intentional - ensure clarity, conciseness, and precision in your requests. Make sure others know what they need to do, when they need to do it, and how you expect the work to be done. The clearer your ask, the better the results you'll achieve. But is there a right or wrong way to ask? Absolutely!

First, understand what you are asking from others. If you're seeking small inputs or help that won't take up much of their time, it's generally okay. However, if you're asking too much of anyone, there's a higher chance of them saying no or not being able to assist you effectively.

Secondly, we shouldn't ask someone to do something they are not suited for. For example, I wouldn't approach a finance person with no graphic design knowledge and ask, "Can you please help me edit this poster?" They would take longer, and the result may not be satisfactory.

The challenge is not about who is good or not, but rather whether you have the right resources, if it aligns with your priorities, and if it's the best use of your time and effort. If it's not, it's best to let others handle these tasks and seek help from those who are more skilled.

Timing is another crucial aspect to consider. Don't assume the other person is available or in the right mindset to understand your request. Always check with them if it's the right time to talk or make a request. If they say no, respect that and come back at a more suitable time or schedule a specific time when they will be free. Ensure they are not preoccupied with numerous thoughts and are genuinely listening to your conversation. If they are distracted, it's best to postpone asking for help, as the chances of receiving it diminish.

Furthermore, don't wait until it's too late to ask, especially when tasks or deadlines are involved. Approaching someone on the day of a deadline and saying, "Hey, I need help with this right now," is not considerate. We can't expect others to drop everything immediately and assist us. Be mindful that they have their own work and responsibilities. Give them a heads up in advance, such as, "I need this by next week. Would you be able to help?" This allows them time and flexibility to support you. Similarly, if you're seeking a promotion at work, don't be like my friend and never ask for it. Also, don't wait until your appraisal meeting. Have those conversations as situations arise or shortly afterward. Waiting until the last minute or when decisions are being made is often too late.

Knocking For Opportunities

Let us say you know what you want to do at work, and it isn't necessarily your defined job, then what? Bow your head and do your work? Absolutely not! Be proactive! Seek opportunities beyond your JD (job description). Set intentions for the kind of work you want to do and ask!

Have you noticed that most of the work we actually do differs significantly from the initial JD provided during the interview process? Many of the tasks we end up performing are not even mentioned in the JD. That is not necessarily a bad thing. If we genuinely want to grow and ace at work, we need to exceed the limits of our JD. The only catch here is to become aware of where and when to stretch the limits. You will not be stopped from doing good work! So, find work that you are more enthusiastic to do and is more aligned with your personal needs.

Where can we find these opportunities, you may ask? Interestingly, it's quite simple. Here are three approaches:

1. Interests:

   If there's a project or task that genuinely interests you, ask to work on it. If what your colleague is doing interests you, ask to help him out and learn the ropes. Get yourself involved in activities of your interest either to learn, help, or explore. Pursuing tasks aligned with your interests is the first step toward doing something you truly enjoy.

2. Support your boss:

   Start taking on tasks that your boss typically handles. Essentially, take over some of your boss's responsibilities. Help your boss, observe their work, provide inputs, and offer information that can assist them in performing their job better. This approach not only allows you to gain visibility for your efforts but also enables you to expand beyond your current role.

3. Initiatives:

   Take initiative and come up with small projects or tasks on your own. Consider what would benefit your team or the company and propose these initiatives to your colleagues or managers. Carve out a little time in your schedule to work on small initiatives. Seek official approval for larger projects or initiatives, as they may become your own pet projects.

Word of caution: It is crucial to remember that you still have your regular work to accomplish. You can't simply pawn off your tasks to others and solely focus on more exciting work and initiatives to go beyond your JD. It's essential to learn how to prioritise your tasks and filter the opportunities you pursue. You can't do everything, so you need to prioritise and determine which initiatives or opportunities make the most sense to work on right now and have the most significant impact on the team. Using such filters helps identify the right opportunities to pursue and move beyond the confines of your JD. More help on this in the upcoming chapters.

The No Fallacy

While it would be wonderful to work on all the new, interesting, and cool things all the time, it's not practically feasible and can lead to burnout. Classic Workaholism! We just don't have enough time or resources to do it all. Other people saying no is a factor too, right? Hence, it is imperative for us to really excel at what we do. We will discuss strategies for how to make these work in the final section of this book. For now, let us address one more nuance to being proactive – learning to say no!

While you are gallivanting away asking for new opportunities, meaningful work, or promotions, others are asking something or the other of you all the time. Given we don't have enough resources, should you really be accepting others' requests?

For many people, including myself, saying no is not easy. We struggle with it because it is driven by underlying fears of what others will think or the fear of losing the opportunity to help. Consequently, it becomes difficult for us to decline requests, and we end up saying yes to many things that don't feel right or overloading ourselves, and worse - neglecting important aspects of our lives such as health, family, or other priorities. Saying yes when we're unable to help, or when it is not in our capabilities, can result in subpar work or strained relationships. Viewing tasks in this way helps us analyse whether we are the right person for the task and if it's the right time for us to help. Knowing that if you don't set your goals and priorities, others will set them for you, it's important to learn how to say no.

When you know you need to say no, say it! It may make you feel weird but there are useful tricks to this trade. Let me help you out with some tips.

Maintain self-respect. You don't have to provide a lengthy explanation for saying no. A simple statement like "I am busy right now" is sufficient. Understand that when you say no, you're not rejecting the person, but simply declining the specific request. (The same applies when they say no, right?) You can make that clear to them. For instance, you could say, "I would love to help you; however, I am currently swamped and unable to take on this request."

One other thing you could do is to help indirectly. You can suggest that while you may not be the right person for the task, there is someone else who is amazing at it and would be a better fit to assist them. This way, you're accepting that there is someone more suitable for the job and giving them credit too. However, be mindful of the communication process. If you act as a communication channel with a third person, ensure that you fully understand the requirements and clearly communicate them. You don't want to get caught in the chain. It's best to let the people involved have direct communication to avoid any miscommunication for which you might be held responsible.

Remember, saying no is about setting boundaries and prioritising your own well-being. It allows you to focus on what truly aligns with your goals and responsibilities. You need to give permission to others to infiltrate your alignment. It is not the other way around.

Nobody needs to give you permission or explicitly tell you to work on new initiatives. These are actions you can take on your own. Be proactive, identify new opportunities, and make a substantial impact on your team and company. This approach will help you be recognised as a high performer and foster significant growth in your job. It's rare to achieve substantial growth within a company by merely performing basic tasks. If you genuinely want to progress, start being proactive.

Chapter Summary

You can decide the course of your career and interactions by being proactive. Be proactive and ask for what you need to make a significant impact on your team and company, and most importantly in your own life.

Key takeaways from this chapter are:

- Being proactive is about asking, setting intentions, and finding opportunities.
- Asking is essential. Whether it's seeking promotions, feedback, or help, you need to be proactive and ask for what you want.
- Building a relationship, being clear about what you want, and being understanding when others say no are crucial aspects of effective asking.
- Be proactive in seeking opportunities that align with your interests and skills. Take initiative, support your boss, and explore tasks beyond your regular responsibilities.
- Saying no is essential to prioritise your own well-being and avoid overcommitting yourself.

Overall, being proactive, identifying opportunities, and taking on initiatives beyond your job description can lead to personal and professional growth and contribute to your success in the workplace.

Owning this work and showcasing it is the next change we will explore. Read on, for manoeuvres on proving your value at work.

Check-In Exercise

At this point in the book, take a moment to check-in with what you take away from this chapter.

- *What aspects of work would you like to control?*
- *How do you rate your openness to ask for what you want on a scale of 1 to 10 (10 being the highest)?*
- *What will you do to increase your score by 1?*

Try the following:

- *Identify ways to seek feedback.*
- *Identify what you can say no to and exercise it in small steps.*
- *Identify what opportunities you can explore at work.*

Chapter Five

Prove Your value

"To find yourself, think for yourself."

–Socrates

Knowing your value is different from showing it. The next change we bring into how we work is to change how we are perceived at work. Don't assume that everybody knows you. To be very honest, I believe that everyone is actually busy in their own lives and caught up in their own troubles, experiences, or thoughts to pay too much attention to anybody else. So, it is up to you to show people what you are capable of and worth.

Do you want to get that promotion at work, make more money, and get interesting projects? Then show your value and prove it to the decision-makers and other people around you. Why? Because first of all, you are not entitled. We discussed this briefly in Chapter 2, and let's go deeper here. During my various coaching conversations, I have come across a few people who say, 'I have been in this role for five years now, it is about time I get promoted.' And I start to burst their bubble, that it is not a given. There is no written guarantee anywhere that if you spend 'x' years in a particular role, you will get promoted to the next one. Moreover, when it comes to bonuses, there are two factors at most – the company performance, and YOUR performance. Furthermore, the way your performance is perceived in the eyes of the decision-makers of the company.

A client once said, "But my boss is pretty good. I know he will be fair and take care of things". And he will! To a large extent, he has a big role in making or breaking your career. But remember being proactive? Only depending on him is not the answer to your desires at work. Hence, it becomes imperative that we take this into our own control and own our work. It's in our best interest, that we stand up for ourselves and prove the value that we bring to the table.

The Value Thing

Now, how do we determine our value? First of all, understand it and know it yourself. When we talk about value, there are two sides to this coin. One is the value that you place on yourself, and the other is the value that the company places on you. If you have done the exercises or gone through the process in chapter three, then you have done the groundwork for determining your own value. What about the value the company places on you? In simplest terms, this is the salary that they pay you or the cost to the company that they incur in keeping you at the company. But a salary doesn't necessarily define your capabilities or your value whatsoever, and we will talk about that further. And not every company is fair or right in the valuation they place on you. You could be more valuable in a different work setting or less valuable in a different one. Every company has a different pay structure and may have a different pay scale. And no one role is necessarily the same in different companies. For example, the role of a system engineer means different things in different companies. That is what makes this tricky.

Hence, get to a point where you do some research - research the market, and understand what a similar job, or a similar job as your role, pays in other companies or averages in the market. Try to find a benchmark job that matches at least 70 to 75% of the kind of work you do, and the skill set required. We do this since no two jobs are alike and it gives you better clarity on the ballpark figure of the value that a company places on its employees.

Having said this, I acknowledge that the value one places on you is not necessarily just about the money they pay you. 'It's not about the salary', you can say. But let's question that. How much you make in a job does not define whether you're good at it or not, or what you're capable of, and I'm totally on board with that! However, you are at your current job because of the money. Unless the answer to the question, "Would you do this job for free?" is yes, you are in it for the money. Money is a big part of it, and if somebody pays you higher than what they are currently paying you, for a similar job, you would probably not bat an eyelid before you make that jump.

So, if you want to grow in your current position or make more money, then you need to increase the value of your work. This doesn't mean you do more work and burn yourself out. But it is about having the right strategy in place.

Quantify

The way to quantify what you bring to the table or the value you have is to determine the impact of your work on the bigger scope of the company, no matter if you're in operations, coding, or IT. How does your work affect the cost or revenue of the company directly? These are numbers that people want to talk about at the senior level. If you are doing work that brings in business or money to the company, then you would have more weightage than somebody who is costing the company more money, right? That way, you understand that your salary isn't just a number, but is actually an inference or a derivative of the company's goals, objectives, and performance as well.

Once you have an understanding of your value, the next question would be: How do you showcase your value? How do you even show it to other people? Not by bragging. Not by exaggeration. You wouldn't (and shouldn't) go around telling everybody, 'I'm an expert at this' or 'I'm very good at this' to their faces all the time. From another perspective, we also find people who are great at making a mountain of a molehill. I have seen people who will do small things and boast about it as if they've done the greatest thing in the world. And that just puts people off! Because a true professional understands who does what without having to be told. If people are not seeing through other people's fluff, you really need to consider the culture or nature of where you are!

Another terrible way I have seen people try to prove their value is to hold on to information. Hold on to intellectual property or hold on to their tasks and not let anybody else know how they do it or what they do! When you hold on to information, it makes you feel like you are in control, you are in power, and that other people have to come to you to get any kind of information and they have to depend on you. You may be holding on to that position, but you won't grow much from there. Simply because no one else can do what you do – so you are stuck doing it all the time! If you really want to grow, you need to start becoming a team player, understanding the dynamics of everything. It makes your life simpler because you don't have to be the only person work depends on. If you are not there, the entire work crashes. That just shows you are a very selfish person and not necessarily a team player.

Be A Brand

What you really need to do to show off your value is to build a brand. Become a brand that people recognise. This is about establishing your expertise and delivering amazing work. You can do all this when you actually own your work and take full responsibility for it. So be a brand and become a person who stands for what you believe in and what you do. So that people would know, whether they know you by name or not, they would know, 'Oh, this person is capable of doing this kind of quality work'. Trust me, a lot more people know me as the girl who made that presentation than they remember my name. (Pragnya Venigalla isn't the most memorable or easy-to-remember name anyway :-p)

Brand building takes time and effort and is something that doesn't come easily to many of us. But what we can do easily is showcase our work in the right light. What do I mean by this? Let's take an example of a performance appraisal meeting. In most places, this is a mere formality – a list of self-scored criteria is re-evaluated and discussed, and an overall number is derived to determine your performance. How do you approach these discussions? Score yourself high because you know your boss is going to downscale them? Or undermine your own efforts and give yourself an okay rating? Either way, you are taking a very subjective approach. What you need to do to prove your value is to become as objective as you can. Let numbers, figures, and outputs drive your ratings. Instead of saying "I have gone above and beyond to deliver on the expectations", try saying "I had zero errors in the deliverable", or "I increased the speed of delivery by 20%". These may sound different in different work settings and roles. The idea is to quantify your efforts. Showcase how your work helped reduce costs (time, money, or resources), or increase revenues. Never discuss the tasks given to you but focus on the outcomes of those tasks.

Many times, it is possible that while engaging in this activity, you understand that the value that you place on yourself or the company places on you isn't necessarily where you want it to be, or you believe that it can be better or there is some scope for improvement. If you think so, I agree. We can never be entirely satisfied, and that's just how we are wired. Our needs and demands keep increasing as we grow, our families grow, priorities change or interests vary, and we need to start making more money. (Inflation doesn't make it any better) It doesn't mean working harder. Also, many times, people think, 'Okay, it's just a matter of time. I will work at this salary for another one or two years and then make a jump or I will get promoted or I'll get a bonus.' But don't wait it out because then you are just leaving things out of your control, and you will feel helpless when things don't turn out the way you want them to. Hence, become proactive in seeking new opportunities or places to showcase your expertise and deliver high-quality work with your skills and capabilities. When we notice a gap between our current value and where we want it to be, that's a perfect place to start. Because now, you can focus on increasing your value.

One way to increase your value is to work on your own skills - skill building. Skill building is essential when it comes to growing the quality of your work and enhancing your own capabilities and skill sets at any point in time. The more skills you have, the more likely you are to get paid more. You can do this in various ways, which we will also discuss in the further sections of this book. Simple examples could be getting more certifications, acquiring degrees, and learning more skills. It doesn't necessarily have to be paid. It doesn't necessarily have to be opportunities that your workplace gives you. There are plenty of free learnings available at our fingertips today. The important thing is to develop an attitude of learning and improving.

Another thing to consider when trying to increase your value is to consider the environment. Let's take an example of a water bottle. It costs a few bucks at the supermarket, is more expensive at entertainment centres (cinemas, adventure parks), and is heavily priced at high-end restaurants. The water didn't change. What changed the value of the water was the environment it was being sold in. Similarly, you may be valued more in a different company or sector. Your presentation skills may not have a life-changing impact during team presentations but will if you are a trainer or public speaker.

When you work on yourself, you prove to yourself and understand what you are bringing to the table and what people can expect from you. You are building your own brand, and brands become valuable. You are then not just turning up at work in a lower energy state, but you actually come feeling good about your work, feeling great about what you're doing, and having constant progress in your life. Be honest, isn't that just the nicest thing to have happened?

Chapter Summary

You can feel you are valuable, but if others don't see it, it won't make any difference to you or your career. It's up to you to demonstrate your capabilities and worth.

Overall, the key takeaways from the chapter are:

- It is important to be objective in performance evaluations and highlight measurable outcomes. Don't assume that others automatically recognise your value. Take proactive steps to prove it.

- Understand and quantify the impact of your work on the company's goals, costs, or revenue. Salary is not the sole indicator of value. Research the market to understand the value of your role.
- Build your personal brand by establishing expertise and delivering outstanding work.
- Take ownership of your work and be proactive in seeking new opportunities.
- Continuously improve your skills through certifications, degrees, and learning.

By determining your own value, showcasing it, and proactively working to increase it, you control the outcomes of your work. To become an Ace at Work, it is up to you to determine how your career shapes out.

Read on to discover how you can make actionable changes at work and approach it in a different way to make your career shine.

Check-In Exercise

At this point in the book, take a moment to check-in with what you take away from this chapter.

- *How valuable do you feel at your work?*

- *How do you rate your value at work on a scale of 1 to 10 (10 being the highest)?*
- *What will you do to increase your score by 1?*

Try the following:

- *Find ways to quantify your results at work.*
- *Identify ways in which you can build your brand.*
- *Identify what you can do to increase your brand.*

Chapter Six

The Way You Work

"Success is liking yourself, liking what you do, and liking how you do it."

–Maya Angelou

- Do you not see the desired results or growth in your career?
- Do you feel like you are working too hard without getting enough out of your job?
- Do you ever feel unrecognised for your efforts?
- Do you have career goals and desires that your current job doesn't seem to fulfil?
- Does your job feel unfulfilling?

Then there is something wrong with the way you work. And what is wrong with what I do, you may ask!

Number one, more often than not, the thought of looking for better opportunities in other companies or switching jobs has crossed your mind.

Number two, work is not making you come alive. Your work doesn't excite you, and it is not something that you actively look forward to. Monday blues are a real thing! Weekends are a real longing. There is something in you that says it could be better.

Number three, most of the time at work is spent on tasks other than your needle-moving tasks. Your active working hours go into firefighting mode, replying to emails, attending meetings, or prioritising other people's needs rather than those that help you progress in your career.

Number four, work stresses you out with dangling deadlines, high-pressure environments, or situations where work never seems to get over and it becomes a never-ending chore.

Number five, you don't see a way out or see another way to do it. If you're constantly doing the same tasks or similar work day in and day out, and you don't see other possibilities or alternative ways to approach your current work.

If any of these have resonated with you or you have said, "Yes, that's me," then there is clearly something wrong with the way you work. But the good news is: We can fix it. You are not doomed to be stuck here. The next logical question to ask is, "How can I work right?" What does that even mean?

Working right means being efficient and effective in the work you do, becoming a productivity superstar, and unleashing your peak performance. It means being in a flow state where work actually makes you feel energised, and hours pass like minutes or moments when you are working on tasks that truly matter. It means feeling fulfilled at the end of the day!

That is the kind of work you need to be doing and want to be working on. That's where the juice is. We will talk about more strategies to enhance our work in part three of this book. But for now, let's start exploring what we can begin with: change. You cannot continue doing what you have been doing and expect different results! You cannot keep showing up the way you have been and expect a miraculous breakthrough.

Now, before any alarms go off in your head about the word "change," no need to worry, because I understand that change can be very uncomfortable. We are wired that way. Our brains start going on an overhaul the moment we try to change anything. Hence, we start with small changes. The little things that don't send us running in the opposite direction!

The first and foremost thing we need to change is our mindset. Whenever we talk about making certain changes in your workplace, I'm sure there's a part of you that starts resisting or rejecting the idea. You might say things like, "Oh, but this idea will not work for me. My situation is different," or "In my kind of workplace, what is being said here absolutely won't work." Or you may find yourself saying, "I don't have time to do all this. I'm so busy at work that I cannot spare any more time than what I already spend on my specific tasks. I'm just too busy. I go in the morning, work till late, and I come back.

I don't even have time to think about all this." Or you find yourself coming up with a list of excuses or thoughts filled with words like "but" "if," "I have to," "should," "must." Know that these voices or thoughts are telling you that you hold certain beliefs about your workplace. It is not wrong to hold beliefs. We all have them, and they stem from our deep subconscious levels. They are deeply ingrained in us through all of our experiences in life. Many times, we aren't even aware of them.

What I'm asking you to do here is not to start making drastic changes in your workplace but simply to start questioning your beliefs. Ask, "Is this really true? Can I be open to this idea and try it to see how it impacts me?" Know that having a balanced, fulfilling, meaningful work-life is possible. Having a career of your dreams is possible. Having work that empowers you is possible. Even for you! No matter the situation, company, industry, or work culture you are in. This is a possibility, and to make it true for you, start becoming aware of your thoughts and expose your beliefs that tell you otherwise.

Not all thoughts and beliefs are wrong or harmful. They drive how we behave or what we do, and the habits that we follow. However, we need to be able to identify the things that we do almost mindlessly and see if these things are helping or hindering our progress. In the previous section of the book, we have excessively discussed the role of awareness in shaping our careers. Start paying attention to what you do on a daily basis at your workplace and in your life, even outside of work. You will immediately start uncovering a treasure chest of behaviours and habits that you don't even realise you have.

This may be a long shot, but a lot of our time is 'wasted' at work with essentially 3 things: Emails, meetings, and distractions. We all intentionally or unintentionally have habits associated with these that can be detrimental to our growth and hinder us from becoming the Ace at work.

Let's explore some work habits that many of us have with respect to these work-wasters, and what we can do to overcome them. These are simple habits that we can easily change with a little bit of intention.

Emails

What is the first thing we do when we switch on our laptops or desktops? A majority of us check our email. This is literally the first thing we do at work, and enough productivity experts and gurus have recommended otherwise. It is not the most efficient or effective way to start your day. When you start your day by checking incoming messages, you are essentially letting external sources dictate your agenda. You're immediately exposed to a barrage of information and tasks, which can overwhelm your brain before you've even had a chance to plan your priorities. Thus, resulting in what is called cognitive overload. And seeing the volume of unread emails or urgent tasks could very easily stress you out or make you anxious. And that feeling sticks with you throughout the day. Not the most optimal way to work, I am sure you agree. Additionally, for many of us, the morning hours are when we are fresh and have more energy than when compared to later. You wouldn't want to spend your high-energy time responding to email! That time should be focused on your priorities. Begin your day by setting intentions, prioritising your tasks, and planning your day. You can get to your beloved email once you have done that!

Another thing to consider is the time you spend on your email and how much it costs you! Cost? Emails are free! Let's debunk that. Let's say you get 100 emails a day. It takes you anywhere between a minute to 5 minutes to check each one. It will take more time than that if the emails are long or require you to respond. But for the sake of a discussion, let's say 2 minutes per email. This amounts to 200 minutes or 3 hours and 20 minutes. In a typical 8-hour workday, that is almost 40% of your day! Further, you were hired at a cost to the company. Let's assume you earn $50000 annually. With a 40-hour work week, it means you get paid approx. $25 per hour. You just cost around $85 on emails per day. Are you sure you were hired to check emails? That is a lot of time and money spent away from the tasks that help make your work more fulfilling and meaningful.

Often, when I discuss this with my clients, I hear them say that email is part of their work. All the work gets done via email. I don't blame them. They are right. By all means, I understand that email is a primary communication medium for most of us, where our work is tracked and where we communicate with people. Don't get me wrong. Emails are super effective in information sharing, coordination, marketing, and promotions. But in reality, are emails the most effective way of communication for our work? And are they used well? I don't believe so. Many times, the practice is to put everything discussed in emails and follow-up on emails. For example, I have seen emails come to me with statements like, 'As discussed over the phone, I am awaiting your reply,' and the sender would mark their boss or reporting manager in CC. When you do this, you are not holding the other person accountable; you are simply playing safe by putting the conversation in an email. The only objective achieved from this is documenting something so that if something goes wrong or if that person has delayed the work, you have an email stating that you followed up, and your boss is copied on it. If your Boss asks you for an update, you can simply say, "But I informed you about it." This is classic escapism.

Other horrendous emails come with subject lines: "Reminder", "Reminder 1", "Reminder 2", "URGENT", etc. This signals that there is a lack of well-defined processes, workflows, or SLAs (Service Level Agreements). Such emails are not going to solve your problem. You would be better off having task managers and processes in place. (A pet project you could implement. Will discuss these more in the third section of this book)

Now, if these are the types of emails you are receiving and sending, there is clearly something wrong. It is an unfortunate culture that has developed in many organisations. If that is the culture of your workplace, it begins with you stopping or reducing the amount of dependency on emails to get work done. I understand that it is difficult, and almost impossible, to change the culture. However, you can start taking small steps to take ownership of your actions and avoid emails becoming the primary tracking mechanism.

It is possible that our work revolves around emails. If that is the case, I urge you to start looking at other ways of communicating your work, such as direct calls or meetings, to avoid excessive reliance on emails. Encourage open discussions and face-to-face interactions to ensure clear understanding and accountability. And definitely avoid sending or replying to those 'safe escape' emails. You are not doing anybody a favour. This is hiding in the system, a concept we have discussed earlier.

Here are a few things you can do to address these challenges and make email effective:

- Send fewer, shorter emails to receive fewer emails.

  Avoid having email chains with ongoing communications in email. You shouldn't be sending emails where people have to scroll down a chain of emails to understand the context of what is written. Use alternatives to email or phone messages to hold somebody accountable and set deadlines. Utilise a task manager where you can input tasks and follow-up on them. Instead of sending an email to Dave saying, "As discussed, please send me the report," enter a task in your task manager with a due date and follow-up once the due date arrives. This way, you reduce unnecessary emails and have better clarity on all the tasks you're working on. Maintaining a task manager or task list also helps offload mental burdens and improves your ability to think.

- Don't mark the entire world in cc. If someone is marked, or even cc'd, on the email, they should be expecting it or have something to do with it. If you get cc'd on emails for no reason, reply to the sender to keep you out of it.
- Unsubscribe from mailing lists that don't serve you. This may be applicable more to personal emails rather than work emails, but nevertheless, a lot of marketing emails or spam fill out inboxes. Utilise inbuilt features of the email platform to filter out messages from reaching your inbox.

Remember, change starts with you. By questioning the way emails are sent and received and challenging the status quo by demonstrating better email habits yourself, you can contribute to creating a healthier work culture. By shifting away from excessive reliance on emails, you can foster a more dynamic and efficient work environment. Small changes in your approach can make a significant difference in your overall work experience and productivity.

Meetings

For many people, a significant portion of their workdays can be consumed by meetings. There are different kinds of meetings with different people and purposes throughout our working days. Although meetings can be effective mechanisms for collaboration, decision-making, brainstorming, project updates, training, and so on, when used ineffectively, they are huge time-wasters. Depending on your role or position in an organisation, the frequency and intensity of meetings differ. However, let's be honest—nobody truly enjoys attending meetings unless maybe they want to avoid doing actual work, or seem busy. When done well, they are great. But much like emails, meeting habits have corrupted workplaces across the globe, are not effectively managed, and are not necessarily the high-priority tasks on your list. But unlike emails, meetings can be costlier affairs. People could ignore your emails, but when they attend a meeting, their time is affected. Email can impact an individual, but a meeting can impact many people at once. A one-hour meeting with ten people essentially costs 10 hours for the whole group!

We find ourselves attending meetings because we were invited to them. We sit through meetings wondering why we were there in the first place. We are physically present there but mentally occupied with other important things to do or wondering about what's for lunch. Or leave them feeling like nothing was accomplished. Many times, I myself have sat through boring presentations, scrolling on my phone or pretending to work on my laptop screen. I am sure you have been to such meetings too. Not all meetings are wasted time, but these kinds are. Unfortunately, most meetings are of these kinds. If this applies to you, consider making changes to the way meetings are held, and challenge the meeting culture in your organisation. There are essentially 2 things you can do to make a radical difference.

1. Don't attend every meeting
2. Develop your meeting facilitation skills

Let me elaborate on these points for better understanding. I don't just want to share information for you to read through it, but actually give you actionable tools that you can implement.

Start questioning every meeting invitation and consider if simpler phone calls or quick chats can achieve the desired outcome. Secondly, question whether your presence is truly required at each meeting. Avoid attending meetings where your presence is not 100% necessary. If the meeting involves decision-making and you are the decision-maker, you may not be able to delegate attendance to others. However, for meetings such as status updates or catch-ups where your presence isn't absolutely necessary, empower those around you or your team members by allowing them to represent the work being done. This not only benefits them by providing visibility and growth opportunities in their own careers but also frees up your time. There is no mandate to attend every meeting you are invited to. You can decline if you are not required.

When organising a meeting, ensure there is a clear agenda outlining what will be discussed, what the purpose of the meeting is, and who the relevant stakeholders are. Let's be upfront about it and clearly communicate them and ensure that everyone in the meeting is aligned on the desired outcomes and is in the power to contribute. Representatives of decision-makers should not be present in meetings where decisions are being made or finalised.

I recently witnessed this in action. I participated in a discussion where an invitation was sent for a weekly meeting for the organisers of an event. A senior member in the group posed a question: "What will be the agenda and how much time will we meet for?". I was surprised to see this message. Not because it was inappropriate, but because I had never exercised such daring in questioning a meeting organiser! The organiser replied with four bullet points to be discussed and mentioned the duration of the call. Needless to say, decisions were reached faster on the listed points, and the meeting ended almost on time. Now, that was a productive meeting! I was impressed. I started following this for every meeting request I received after this experience. I wouldn't attend if there is no agenda, or if my role is not clear in the meeting! But I would make my absence clear to the meeting organiser, rather than leaving them wondering!

To keep meetings focused and efficient, maintain strict adherence to the agenda, allocating specific time limits for each speaker. Monitor the progress of the discussion and ensure it is moving toward the desired outcome. If the discussion starts to deviate or get off track, it is your responsibility as the meeting organiser to redirect the conversation or park it for future discussion. Assign action items to individuals to address those discussions outside of the meeting. Follow-up with the minutes of the meeting afterward without fail.

Another brilliant meeting practice I observed is to avoid giving context during the meeting. For status meetings, consider providing status updates in the meeting invite itself or through an email. Send out reports or presentations ahead of time.

This way, participants can review the project or report's status beforehand and be prepared for the meeting. The meeting can focus on discussion rather than lengthy presentations. Honestly, most presentations are text-overloaded and boring. Very few presenters take the time to make presentations engaging and worth your time.

Remember, the ultimate goal is to achieve the desired outcomes of the meeting. Any disruptions or distractions should be managed with that in mind. Sometimes, you may have senior participants in the meeting, and you might feel hesitant to assert control. However, when you have a clear agenda and you are driving the meeting, everyone will already know their place in the meeting. Hence, setting clear guidelines for the meeting can be very powerful. Learn to be assertive. You can always say, "With due respect, this topic is outside the scope of this particular meeting", or "Can we schedule a separate meeting to discuss this further". Your communication skills get tested when you are a facilitator. Irrespective of a person's seniority, everyone in the meeting would want to succeed. Nobody likes to waste their time. Always bring people back on track in a meeting. Reconsider inviting some people if they are the constant disruptors.

Having said this, be aware that everyone is different. Some people love to talk and hog up the entire time. Some people will not speak a word. Some want to get attention. Some want to sit at the back quietly. As a meeting facilitator, make sure that if they are in the room, they know what is expected of them. A good facilitator knows how to handle these different types of people. Spend time improving your skills first.

When you start setting boundaries in a meeting, showing up in control, and developing yourself, you will spearhead a culture change. This type of work culture benefits everyone involved.

Distractions

Distractions are inevitable in different types of workplaces. It is one thing to say that you don't have a private space or silence around you to focus. But even if you have a private office with noise-cancelling walls, you can still get distracted by your own thoughts or, more frequently, by the ubiquitous presence of smartphones. In this world of pings and dings, being focused has become a rarity. This affects our work more than we think.

I am not proud of it, but I am a phone addict! Constantly checking messages, or when overwhelmed, doom-scrolling social media sites! I used to believe this is 'normal'. In retrospect, every time I have made major strides, my phone was not part of that scenario! This made me realise my own addiction and forced me to take steps, small and drastic, to deal with it. From switching off my phone during work to setting app timers! I have tried it all!

I challenge you to reflect on your own 'addiction' or dependency on your phones. To get a clearer understanding, look into your phone settings. Most smartphones can give you statistics on your usage which can be very eye-opening. How many times did you unlock your phone today? What

Apps did you use the most? At what times did you use your phone the most?

There is a high probability that you are on your phone, even during busy times of your work throughout the day. I am sure you can spot these phone users around you too. I am guilty too of browsing the net, watching videos, or scrolling through social media during office hours. I was taking a break, I told myself. Sometimes, I was! Sometimes, it was unintentional! Distraction!

A client approached me and complained about not being able to focus and get things done as he was frequently disturbed by calls throughout the day. He even went on to narrate an incident when someone called him with a silly query while he was working on a very important report, and he lost his track. My immediate question to him was, "Why did you answer the phone if you were working on something important?" We all do this, don't we? Our phones have become a constant companion. But here's the thing: Every time we respond to a ping, ding, notification, or call, we are essentially distracted from what we are doing.

And distractions are costly. It is commonly cited in many books that it has been found that it takes up to 15 minutes for a person to regain focus after being distracted. Just imagine, with constant distractions spread throughout our day, how many 15 minutes we lose!

When you are engaged in important tasks, it is essential to focus. Keep distractions at bay. Keep that phone aside. "Wait! But I get calls for work! We would miss important calls!"

Let's be clear on one thing. I am not saying don't use your phone at all! But during blocks of time when you are working on important tasks that need attention, put your phone on silent. Even if it is for an hour! You can always return the calls later or schedule your work during periods when you are less likely to be interrupted. If you missed any calls, you could always call them back and explain that you were held up. You could set-up auto-responders on your phone that send a message to the caller saying you are busy at the moment and will call them back as soon as possible. Nowadays, phones even come with features like Do Not Disturb, where you can set exceptions to allow calls from specific individuals. Limit the number of people whose calls you answer during your designated focus times. Use your phone's settings well.

People walking up to you during your focus blocks are a form of distraction too. Consider working from private spaces or meeting rooms if you have access to them or put up Do Not Disturb signs at your desk when you don't want to be interrupted. Wearing noise-cancelling headphones works too.

Furthermore, many of us even tend to check our email 100 times a day. We are so worried about missing important emails that we constantly check emails in between work or in every free pocket of time. This habit essentially breaks our focus 100 times a day, distracts us, and makes us less productive overall. Have pockets of time dedicated to checking email, spread out throughout the day depending on your work's dependency on emails. Typically, it suffices to check your emails once or twice during the day. During those dedicated pockets of time, you can open your email, check and reply to whatever needs to be addressed, and then switch it off and move on with your other needle-moving tasks.

Distractions can be dealt with only when you become aware of your distractions. Start by paying attention to when you are getting distracted. What triggers cause it? Was the distraction external or internal? What were you doing when you got distracted? Once you identify your sources of distractions and what caused them, you can deal with them with a little bit of intention. Awareness and intention can go a long way in dealing with the various distractions around work.

Way Ahead

So far, we have discussed how some of the biggest 'time-wasters' affect us and how we can deal with them. That is a great place to start to rethink the way you work. Even without the time-wasters, we can still enhance our effectiveness by developing some healthy work habits.

Maintaining clarity about your tasks and priorities is one of them. Begin each day by identifying the tasks you need to accomplish and ensure they align with your personal priorities as well as those of your reporting manager or team. If you're unsure about your priorities, utilise prioritisation techniques to determine what they might be. Some popular prioritisation techniques are as follows.

- The **Eisenhower Matrix technique** categorises tasks into four quadrants based on their urgency and importance. Urgent and important tasks should be done immediately. Important, but Not Urgent tasks can be scheduled for later. Urgent, but non-important tasks can be delegated if possible. Consider eliminating or postponing Neither Urgent nor important tasks.

- The **ABCD Method** involves labelling tasks as A, B, C, or D based on their priority. A Tasks are High-priority tasks that are important and need to be done as soon as possible. B-Tasks are tasks that are important but not as time-sensitive as A tasks. C Tasks are tasks that are less important and can be done when time permits. D Tasks are those that are to be delegated if possible or consider dropping them.

- **MoSCoW Method** categorises tasks into four categories. Must-Haves are critical tasks that are non-negotiable and must be completed. Should Have tasks are important tasks but not as critical as Must Have. Could Have tasks are Desirable tasks but not essential. Won't-Have (this time) are tasks that can be postponed or dropped for now.

- With an **Impact vs. Effort Matrix,** plot tasks on a graph with impact on one axis and effort on the other. Focus on tasks that have high impact and low effort.

No matter which technique you use to prioritise your tasks, it is essential you do it. If nothing is a priority, then everything becomes a priority. You will end up firefighting and running from task to task with little to no outcome. Overwhelm, burnout, stress are all a result of not having prioritisation in place.

Additionally, have regular sit-downs with your boss to discuss the tasks they expect you to complete or work on. If you have multiple tasks at hand, it's okay to ask for their order of priority. For example, if you have ten tasks, determine the most important one. If your boss assigns you a new task, make it clear that you are currently working on Task X, which is your top priority. Ask if the new task supersedes this priority. If it does, adjust your task list; accordingly, if not, continue working on your current tasks.

I saw a colleague of mine do this and was blown away by how effective he was in negotiating for his time at work with our boss. He would explicitly print out a list of his tasks and show it to our manager during the status update meetings. If a new task got assigned to him, he would ask our manager to number the task. Sometimes task #1 became #2 to accommodate the new task, and sometimes, the new task just got added to the bottom of the list. My colleague outlined how long each task would take and when he would deliver it. All work was looked at as a negotiation. My manager was happy as work got done, and my colleague was happy he left work on time every day. On absolute crisis days, he stayed! But he made it a point to clearly highlight it! He worked in the same high-pressure environment we all did! It baffled me! But I realised that his approach was very simple, and anyone could do it! It didn't disappoint me when I tried it for myself.

The T Factor

This book wouldn't be a productivity book if I didn't address the topic: Time! When I would work, I felt I needed more time in my days! When I had time, I realised I needed more – discipline, clarity, and efficient estimation. This helped me change my worldview: "I don't have time".

To enhance your productivity, consider utilising some simple tools to help manage your time. Keep track of your time. A time log will help you understand how much time you spend on specific tasks. Many companies require employees to track their time and submit reports detailing their work hours. If your company doesn't provide a time tracking system, create one for yourself as it is a useful tool.

As also mentioned in the earlier parts of this chapter, maintain a task list that is distinct from your emails since emails are not effective task holders unless you convert them into tasks within your task manager.

However, merely tracking your time and tasks won't take you far. It's crucial to reflect and review the data you've gathered. Analyse the information and gain clarity about your most time-consuming tasks and how long each task takes. Look for patterns or behaviours that emerge in your workplace. Sometimes you'll notice certain tasks taking longer at specific times of the day when you are not at your best. Let me explain. I would spend hours preparing reports if that is something I did post-lunch. But the same report would get done in less than an hour if it was done just before wrapping up my day at work. The after-lunch slump time was my bottleneck! I would keep my most useless tasks for that period of time. Can you guess what I do in those times? Check emails and reply to WhatsApp messages! Creative work was kept for mornings. Routine tasks for later in the day. This system of categorising work throughout the day worked wonders!

By observing these patterns in your own working behaviours, you can identify which tasks are more suitable for specific times of the day. Analyse the logs with the perspective of whether all the tasks you worked on this week align with your overall objectives and the expectations of your reporting manager.

When you start analysing these reports, you'll discover areas where you can improve efficiency, reduce wasted time, increase focus, or eliminate unnecessary tasks altogether. By re-evaluating your work and tasks retrospectively, you will be better equipped to plan your future activities. Taking ownership of your work and domain will make you stand out in the workplace, and it's only a matter of time before you are recognised for your outstanding performance.

Chapter Summary

Considering job changes, lack of enthusiasm for work, spending time on non-essential tasks, work-related stress, and limited possibilities for change are all indicators of misalignment in our wants and needs and our actual work.

By addressing the way, we work, we can overcome many of these and carve a path for our career fulfilment.

Overall, the key takeaways from the chapter are:

- Reflect on your work and tasks to identify areas of improvement, reduce time wastage, and increase focus.
- Meetings and emails can be significant time-wasters. Changing email habits, attending fewer meetings, and handling distractions effectively are ways to enhance productivity.
- Reduce dependency on email by dedicating specific time slots for checking and responding to emails. Explore alternative communication methods, such as direct calls or meetings, to avoid excessive reliance on email.
- Evaluate the necessity of meetings, set clear agendas, and invite only relevant stakeholders to meetings to ensure focused and productive discussions.
- Minimise distractions from smartphones during work by keeping them aside or utilising built-in features.
- Track your time and review the data to identify time-consuming tasks and patterns for better planning and optimisation.
- Align your work with personal priorities and the expectations of your reporting manager. Regular communication helps clarify task priorities.

By taking ownership of your work and thoughtfully managing your tasks, you can stand out in the workplace, which will help you achieve a fulfilling and meaningful work-life. It is the way we approach work that needs to shift.

In the further section of this book, we will explore what you can achieve with this redefined definition of work and time.

Check-In Exercise

At this point in the book, take a moment to check-in with what you take away from this chapter.

- *What are the tasks that consume most of your time?*
- *How do you rate your time management skills on a scale of 1 to 10 (10 being the highest)?*
- *What will you do to increase your score by 1?*

Try the following:

- *Identify time blocks for email and for ways to eliminate unnecessary emails.*
- *Set meetings with clear agendas and instructions for attendees.*
- *Identify ways you can leverage your phone's settings for better focus.*

Part III

Excel

"If we did the things, we are capable of doing, we would literally astound ourselves."

–Thomas Edison

With so much to do, we can easily lose our footing. Going the extra mile at work isn't about overworking, burning out, or losing yourself. It is about making significant impacts and getting noticed. This is the essence of becoming an Ace at Work.

This section of the book explores out-of-the-box thinking and finding solutions that not just transform the way you work but also change the nature of your work. If you have reached this far into the book, I am sure of one thing about you – that you have it in you to do it! To excel at work! This entails gaining a bigger picture of the impact of your work and streamlining your tasks to propel work that matters and gets noticed.

Career growth doesn't happen by chance. It happens with intentional directed efforts towards common goals. It happens through thoughtful work. And in these final chapters, we will explore exactly that! Pull up your socks and head down a path of rethinking work in new dimensions!

Chapter Seven

Get Relationships to Work

"It's only after you've stepped outside your comfort zone that you begin to change, grow and transform."

–Roy T. Bennet

I think by now you will definitely understand that you don't work alone or that you can't really grow if you are working all by yourself without the support of people. For starters, that would also question our very existence because we humans are social animals. It is often said that your network is your net worth, and that is what we will focus on in this chapter—how we can build our network and how we can get our relationships to work for us. Don't expect immediate results. This process requires work, patience, persistence, and an attitude to serve.

Now, a question arises: Who should I build relationships with? I already have amazing friends and a big group or circle. Who do I need to approach to grow in my career? The answer to this is simple. Are the people in your circles or your network or your friends helping you grow in your career? Are they discussing goals and ideas with you and helping you fast forward your growth? If not, start relooking at your circles. It is said that we become the average of the five people that we hang around with. Are your friends the kind of people you want to become or the kind of people who are just stopping you from becoming who you can be? I am not saying break ties with friends who don't help you grow (Though breaking away from toxic relationships isn't such a bad thing). Har ek friend *zaroori* hota hain. Every kind of friend is necessary. But never stretch yourself too thin to keep in touch with EVERYBODY, and not have any energy for yourself. It helps to be very intentional about who it is that we want to keep in our inner circle and build strong relationships with.

Being specific to building relationships at work, there could be many people who play a role in how your career spans out. But a common person across everyone's list is your manager. He or she is the one person who can make or break your career. The likelihood of you sticking around with a bad boss is very low. But a good boss doesn't mean you will stick around too. An article published by Harvard Business Review on Why People Really Quit Their Jobs1 highlights that people didn't quit because of a good or bad boss. People left when their job wasn't enjoyable, their strengths weren't being used, and they weren't growing in their careers, but the managers are the ones who are responsible for what the job is like! Hence, it becomes important for us to build good relationships with our managers.

Another person(s) who could potentially spearhead your career growth is your super boss or the manager's manager. They, or other people in senior management in your company, are the next level of relationships that you need to build to ensure a platform that lets you excel at work. Why is this important? Because these are the people who are the actual decision-makers. Their decisions or their perceptions are what shape your career growth. It also helps you get visibility of your work and your capacities and skills. It ensures that your career growth isn't just dependent on your manager, which can be highly risky. After all, has it ever occurred to you that your manager may be in the same boat as you are? If you have ever considered changing your job, don't you think they also have? Hence, it always helps that other people can root for you too.

The next bracket of people we need to build relationships with are our colleagues—people that we work with, people in our team, people who are around us at work. These are the people who may not necessarily fuel your career growth, but they are very crucial for you to get the necessary help and support in doing your work.

Furthermore, if you are in a client-facing job, the client relationships are the ones you need to get a hold of. If you have clients who are open to discussing things with you, are transparent with you, and are those with whom you can be open and transparent, your life becomes easier. It reduces a lot of stress and avoids a lot of escalations and pressures that arise from these situations. Now, it's not always that clients are bad people. However, clients are very understanding if you have a good relationship built with them.

A client I once had while in the role of a Relationship Manager would always come to me for any issues. Delays, things they were upset with, and requests they needed to make, all came to me directly. They were very comfortable with me and trusted that I would help them. Not once did a call or email go to my manager saying I was not responding to them. This was because I spent a lot of time building a relationship with them. Spending a lunch break with them talking about things apart from work can go a long way.

Last but not least, you need to have good relationships with mentors. First, sidebar: if you don't have a mentor, get one. They are the ones who help speed up your learning and guide you on your path. Mentors are people who have gone through your journey and people who truly know and understand what you are going through in terms of growth and learning.

Working Relationships

The next question that arises is: What kind of relationships should I build with these people? You don't need to be BFFs with everyone. You don't need to start inviting them for dinner parties or family functions. You just need working relationships. This is different from relationships at work. Working relationships are those where conversations get deeper, problems get discussed, and healthy, open, transparent communication is encouraged. It is where you can share your wants and needs, dreams and desires, challenges and struggles, and be helpful to each other.

One of the most important and impactful working relationships you must have is with your manager. Imagine being able to talk to your manager about what kind of work you want to be doing, and he responds openly and not always dangling carrots in front of you or making false promises about promotions or hikes. You want to be able to see beyond statements like “I will get back to you”, “Let me see what I can do”, or “I am speaking to the upper management”. A working relationship with your boss is where he gives you the correct picture. Frequent, open, transparent communication is one aspect for sure. What also makes a working relationship with a manager is being able to garner feedback – not just during an annual appraisal, but month-on-month, week-on-week. The conversations between your manager and you should be focused on how you are progressing and how you can improve. This helps you implement all of the change concepts discussed in previous chapters.

With all other categories of identified relationships to build too, the goal is to be mutually helpful and supportive – through open communication and regular feedback.

A simple thing to understand is to draw boundaries—boundaries of where and when you would be able to engage with this person. You cannot approach the CEO of a company or a superior in your management and start talking about your troubles at home. It puts them off and wastes a lot of their time as well. Don’t discuss problems with your senior bosses; instead, discuss solutions and ideas—that's where it will be advantageous for you.

Further, let's talk about the kinds of relationships we don't want to have.

Number one: **Gossip.**

Don't build relationships based on gossiping about each other because when somebody gossips to you, it can also mean that they will gossip about you to somebody else. That doesn't help build a healthy work atmosphere.

Another thing to steer away from is **Politics**.

Stop getting in other people's way. Remember that everybody is on your side and is just trying to help you. It won't benefit you or anyone else if you engage in workplace politics and start sabotaging each other's careers. Try to have a mindset of inclusivity and collaboration, not competition.

And a definite no-no when it comes to building relationships is **Bootlicking!**

Just buttering up your boss, complimenting them about everything they do, or being a yes-man! Not just with your boss, but anybody for that matter. It's not a healthy relationship. They will just keep you around because their ego is satisfied, and it won't go beyond that.

Also, don't become too Salesy. Don't start approaching people with a desperate "I need something from you" mentality. They won't be inclined to help you unless they know you, your capabilities, skills, and background. Don't have underlying agendas of wanting to build a relationship with someone because they are going to help you with something. No! They could end up feeling cheated, and all your efforts would backfire. Build relationships without expecting anything from them.

Building Relationships

Many times, it's possible that we want to connect with people who are not necessarily in our immediate circle or contacts. We don't know these people, or we don't have access to them. How do we start building relationships with them? **Networking.** We live in a very digitally connected world, and one of the easiest ways to start connecting with such people is to ask for a reference. If you know somebody who knows the person you want to connect with, start building relationships with them and then ask them to introduce you to the person in the end. Referrals are great. But again, remember: Be nice! Unless you build genuine relationships without underlying agendas, you won't even get that referral. And you never know, help will come to you in various ways if your intentions are pure. The world works in mysterious ways.

If you don't find anybody, there is always LinkedIn to the rescue. LinkedIn connections are underused by most of us. We don't truly understand the power of LinkedIn and what it can bring to the table. You can send connection requests to anybody in the world as long as they are on LinkedIn, and most working professionals would have a profile there.

One point to remember though, is when you are connecting with somebody, when you're approaching somebody (even in person), try connecting over common ground. When you see somebody's profile and notice that they have worked in a certain company, for example, try reaching out to them saying, "Hey, I see you have worked at this company, and I have worked there too. It's surprising that we have never crossed paths". Don't be too cheesy and stalk them. Be open and transparent.

When we approach people, we don't approach them with an attitude of asking for help, but with an attitude to learn from them or by reaching out to help them. Everybody loves to teach others, and when you approach somebody with an attitude of "I'm not greater than you, but I want to learn from you because you inspire me", it makes them feel good about themselves and you. And when you help them, your help will come back to you in different ways.

When I say, "help them," try to solve a problem for them, get to know them, understand the challenges they're going through or what is on their mind, and try to do simple things that can take a little bit of their problems off the table. If they are struggling with some PowerPoint features, lend your expertise in helping them in their presentation. If they are unable to finish a task by a looming deadline, and you can spare some time, then offer to help out. Fill in for them when they are stuck or unable to attend a meeting. Working relationships don't have to be about work. If someone is dealing with the stress of house-shifting, connect them with some movers you are aware of. If someone wants to go on a vacation but is struggling with the planning, help them figure out the logistics of their travel. Your experience and connections can be leveraged massively in helping people solve small problems.

When you do that, you are serving them. Serve with all your heart and mind and be very intentional about doing this without any ulterior motives. I can't stress this enough. It's not about cheating them; you're just trying to help them. Sometimes, we may wonder, "Why would this person even talk to me or why would they help me in the future?" Because we are not asking, but we are giving. Remember, don't have expectations, just help with the intention of building relationships, and don't expect that relationship to turn into something significant right away.

Remember to be open-minded. People are different; they come from diverse backgrounds and have different thoughts, processes, and perspectives about life. Their experiences may differ from yours. So, be open to their thoughts, beliefs, and values. When you reach out to them, don't approach it with the mindset of "I am like this." Just because people are different from you doesn't mean you cannot build relationships with them. Be open to whoever they are and look at them as people and potential friends you want to have in your network. We need to become aware of our own blockers and start accepting other people for who they are. Adapt according to the person you're reaching out to.

A concept from improvisational theatre called "Yes, and" can be applied to networking and relationship building. In an unscripted scene, when someone says something, the second person needs to accept it and add to it. This builds on each other's concepts and fosters a positive connection. This tool can be powerful in networking. Instead of rejecting or judging other people's ideas or thoughts, accept them and say, "Okay, so with that, where can we go?"

You would know what their thoughts and ideas are if you listen! Listening is one of the most important aspects of building relationships. Why? Because most of us listen to reply, not to understand. Don't tell me you have never done that! Listening is a skill that takes practice, patience, and intention. When building relationships, don't just talk, but listen. Let the other person share and ask questions to show genuine interest. When you listen attentively, people will open up to you in ways you may not have imagined. This opens doors for further relationship building and effective communication.

To bring it all together, build genuine relationships with those who can have a significant role to play in your career growth.

- Be open and transparent.
- Have an attitude of learning and helping.
- And listen!

All these things lay the foundation for effective working relationships.

Once you have established a working relationship with someone, you will gradually start showing your value. During relevant discussions or conversations, when it is right, highlight your skills, experiences, or thoughts. Start solving others' problems in turn showcasing your skills and expertise. This doesn't have to be pushy! When people know you and recognise your capabilities, they will automatically consider you for opportunities. It may seem like a lot of work, but when you approach relationships with a genuine desire to learn and help others, you are building authentic connections that can extend beyond the relationship and fuel your personal and professional growth.

Keep the right people around you in the right way. It takes patience, persistence, and practice, but it is worth it.

Chapter Summary

Building relationships in both personal and professional life is significant for career growth. Building genuine relationships by helping others and being open-minded, without underlying agendas, is the way to approach this aspect of our work.

Overall, the key takeaways from the chapter are:

- Having working relationships characterised by open, transparent, and healthy communication is very important.
- Specific relationships to nurture include those with managers, superiors, colleagues, clients, and mentors. Boundaries should be maintained when approaching different people for various purposes.

- Connect over common ground and show interest in the other person's background and experiences.

- Negative relationship behaviours to avoid include gossip, politics, and bootlicking.

- Networking, referrals, and LinkedIn connections can be valuable for building relationships.

- Approach relationships with an attitude of learning and helping. Approach them with genuine intentions and avoid hidden agendas.

Building and maintaining the right relationships takes patience, persistence, and practice but is highly rewarding. Remember, building meaningful relationships requires authenticity, serving others, and a long-term perspective. Surround yourself with the right people and learn how to keep them in your network.

In the next chapter, you will explore how you can leverage these relationships to align your personal tasks to greater objectives.

Check-In Exercise

At this point in the book, take a moment to check-in with what you take away from this chapter.

- *What can be achieved by having working relationships?*

- *How do you rate your relationships at work on a scale of 1 to 10 (10 being the highest)?*

- *What will you do to increase your score by 1?*

Try the following:

1. *Make a list of people you want to build relationships with.*
2. *Identify ways to reach out and learn from these people.*
3. *Identify what skills you can use to help those on your list.*

Chapter Eight

Get Onto What Matters

"It's what you learn after you know it all that counts."

–John Wooden

When you do your work, there is always a set of expectations involved! Expectations that you have from work or others, and expectations others have from you too. An absolutely crucial aspect of excelling at work is setting expectations and clarifying those expectations with all the stakeholders involved. What do I mean by this? When we talk about stakeholders, we are referring to all the people who are impacted by your work. Professionally, they are those who hire you, those who work with you, or those whom you serve – your clients or customers. Personally, they can be your family and friends. They all have certain expectations from you, and you from them.

The real challenge is when these expectations are not explicitly communicated or discussed openly all the time. This can especially be the case if you've been with a company for a while.

Things are moving along. Work is almost a routine. People around you know a bit about you as a person and how you work. You know the people around you and who you can ask for help or guidance or even delegate work to. Work is in a way, fine! This is your comfort zone. It may have been a while since you last discussed expectations or had regular performance appraisal meetings. While these discussions do happen, maybe they don't occur as frequently as they should, or are not as fruitful as they could be. Ever felt like an appraisal could have gone better? Ever wished you could set better goals at work? Ever felt like something was unfair to you? You are not alone! That is why we need to clarify expectations.

What do we clarify? We clarify what we expect when we ask for help, as discussed briefly in the previous chapter. We clarify what we expect when we delegate work. More about this in the next chapter. Here, we will address expectations that others have from us. Formally, these can be goals, objectives, targets, SLAs, KPIs, or KRAs. These are different terminologies you may have come across in your career. The knack is to understand the expectations that go beyond just these! To truly Ace at work, it isn't enough to just do your work. Going the extra mile is a sure-shot way to get noticed and fast-track your growth.

Performance Metrics

Let's understand the role that these formal metrics play in our work.

Goals are an aim or a desired result. Workplace goals can vary widely, encompassing areas such as sales targets, project deadlines, cost reduction objectives, employee performance benchmarks, customer satisfaction scores, and more. These goals are often set in consultation with management, and regular reviews and feedback help ensure that employees are on track to meet them. Their role is to generally serve in providing direction, focus, measurement, and accountability. Let us consider an example to understand this and all the following metrics better. Let's consider a scenario within the marketing department of an e-commerce company. A goal can be increasing online sales by 20% in the next year.

Objectives are essentially the actionable steps that need to be taken to reach overarching goals. These are more specific, concrete, and measurable milestones set to achieve the overarching goals. They are instrumental in helping employees and teams stay focused and motivated, providing a roadmap for what needs to be accomplished. In our example, this can be launching a new marketing campaign or expanding the product catalogue.

Targets are specific, quantifiable goals or objectives set to achieve desired results. Targets are often used to provide more granular and measurable steps toward accomplishing larger objectives or goals. They serve as intermediate steps in the process of reaching larger organisational goals and can be adjusted or modified as circumstances change or new information becomes available. In our example, this can be to develop and finalise the marketing campaign plan within the next 2 months.

SLA stands for Service Level Agreement. It is a formal contract or agreement between a service provider and a customer that defines the level of service expected from the provider. SLAs are commonly used in various industries, including IT, telecommunications, customer support, and outsourcing, to ensure that services are delivered at an acceptable and consistent quality. SLAs are crucial for ensuring that services meet the needs and expectations of the customer. They provide a framework for accountability, transparency, and performance management. An example SLA for our scenario could be the marketing team committing to responding to customer inquiries within 24 hours of receipt.

KRAs, or Key Result Areas, are used to define the primary areas of responsibility and performance expectations for employees, where an individual is expected to focus their efforts to achieve the key results crucial for the success of that role or the organisation as a whole. KRAs are commonly used in performance management, goal setting, and job descriptions. They help employees and managers understand the most important aspects of their roles and how their performance will be evaluated. For a Digital Marketing Manager, a KRA could be generating a 30% increase in website traffic through marketing campaigns. For a Product Manager, a KRA could be adding 500 new product listings to the catalogue.

KPIs, or Key Performance Indicators, are specific metrics or quantifiable measures used to evaluate the performance and success of an organisation, department, project, or individual in achieving their goals and objectives. KPIs serve as a tool for performance management, allowing organisations to monitor progress, set targets, and make data-driven decisions. For the Digital Marketing Manager, a KPI could be the website traffic growth rate. For a Product Manager, a KPI could be the number of new product listings added.

All of these metrics can vary widely from one job to another and from one organisation to another. It is important to understand your metrics. If these are explicitly stated in your job, then you are one step ahead! If these are not explicitly stated, start having discussions about these, or propose your own as per your understanding of your role. Understand them well, and align your activities and tasks towards them. See how these can be improved to make your work more aligned.

You may face situations where you may not necessarily be fully involved in setting these for yourself. Many times, the ones that have been set may not even align with the reality of the work you are doing. I remember once I had KPIs set for me at the beginning of the year, but throughout the year, things kept happening, and the nature of my work kept changing. By the end of the year, I realised that I never even worked on my actual KPIs. Other tasks kept taking up my time and becoming a priority, causing my KPIs to change over time. However, on paper, they still remained the same, and that was what my 'performance' was essentially evaluated on. Needless to say, you can imagine the appraisal discussion at the end of the year! I only discovered ways to handle the performance expectations in these dynamic roles later in my life, and this is what I uncover in the later part of this chapter.

Here is a disclaimer: I am not disregarding formal appraisal systems or performance metrics. I think they are very beneficial and mandatory for people to align with the central aspirations of the company. I do feel, however, that we as employees need to learn to make it work within the varying appraisal cultures that differ from company to company.

The idea of understanding the formal expectations from you - your goals, objectives, targets, KPIs, and KRAs - is to understand what matters and what gets measured. But the needle doesn't stop there. Ever been in a situation where you aced your personal goals, KRAs, KPIs, etc., but still had a lousy appraisal because the department didn't do so well, or the company didn't do so well? Exigencies and things way beyond our control aside, there is a lot we can do to not be in such situations. The key to becoming an Ace at work is to focus on and start working on things that truly matter to you, your team, your department, and your company as a whole. Work on the REAL performance metrics.

The Real Performance Metrics

How will we get to know what matters?

I'm not referring to office gossip, rumours, or water cooler chats. Instead, I'm talking about paying attention to priority projects and activities that are escalating or involving senior management. These are the objectives, tasks, or projects that extend beyond your own responsibilities. They represent the department's priorities at any given time. To gain insight into the tasks that senior employees are focusing on, it's beneficial to have foresight. This information may or may not be readily available. However, if you pay attention to your surroundings and expand your thinking beyond your own work, you will gather a wealth of information.

Pay attention to what is getting attention! Frequently, we find ourselves in situations where we start a project but then get asked to set it aside and work on something else. Why? Have you ever given it a moment's thought? This is where our thinking needs to expand. Priorities change all the time, and we need to be intentionally onboard the tasks that are gaining traction and visibility. Am I asking you to take on more work? Not necessarily! What I am saying is to negotiate your work so that you get to work on the top priorities. Essentially, you need not be told what your priorities are; you learn from observing your seniors and offer to work on them.

Furthermore, start looking at the bigger picture outside of your work. We often focus on our tasks and what we need to do, but rarely do we reflect on the impact of our work on the team, department, or company. Often, we are firefighting at work. If things are getting escalated, that is where the focus shifts! If a deadline is looming, pressure mounts towards that. If work emergencies occur, we tend to them first. If you constantly find yourself firefighting, dealing with one issue after another without a clear sense of importance, it may indicate that you are being short-sighted in your career path and work impact. In all of this, we tend to lose focus on the bigger picture. We can gain this perspective simply by asking, is this 'fire' aligned with the team, department, or company goals and priorities? This makes us question our work!

When we begin to pay attention to the bigger picture, it adds more meaning to our work and changes how we perceive it. This highlights the importance of our work. If we do this, we understand the consequences of not doing it well and how it affects the team. A bonus is that while the entire world is firefighting, you can remain the calm one, focused on the end goals! Thus, driving not just your performance but that of the teams too.

For this to happen, it is effective to build and nurture relationships. We discussed this in the previous chapter. Developing stronger relationships allows people to open up and share critical information with you. Express openly your desire to contribute more to the team and work on important projects. Engaging in such discussions with your manager aligns goals and ensures you are on the same page. They may be focusing on different activities that they deem important, and unless you ask or have these conversations, you won't know. The same applies if you manage a team of people too!

It's rare for a manager to refuse someone who expresses a desire to take on more crucial work unless there is a lack of trust or confidence in your abilities. Hence, it is crucial to first ensure that you are fulfilling your current responsibilities. If you are not delivering on your current obligations and are already asking for additional work, you will not be trusted, and there is a high chance that your manager will reject your request.

I understand that managing priorities can be challenging, especially in high-workload environments. However, I have witnessed remarkable examples of individuals who openly discuss their current tasks with their managers and determine the focus areas for the upcoming week or month. Breaking down objectives into weekly and monthly meetings with periodic reviews can greatly streamline this process.

Start by creating a list of all the activities you are currently engaged in. Evaluate these tasks based on their importance and urgency for the team, company, department, and so on. Involve your manager in these decision-making processes, as they likely have a broader perspective of things. Once your tasks are prioritised, you can look at how much of it is the 'real performance metric'. Awareness about this will give the necessary discussion points. Schedule time to work on the priority tasks and stay on top of the team focus shifts.

At this point, you may be wondering, "I'm already overworked and exhausted." Now we're talking about adding more important and priority work. Won't that increase your workload even further? This just sounds like too much work! Your plate is already full. I hear you! If you have completed the activities and exercises from the previous chapter, you should realise by now that a significant portion of your time is spent on non-critical tasks or tasks that do not align with the direction you want to take. Therefore, it's time to optimise your actions and focus on what truly matters.

Up until this point in the book, we have discussed various strategies on how to align ourselves with our objectives and desires from our jobs and to map out our desired direction. If what we are currently doing does not align with that path, it is necessary to make small changes and tweaks in our approach. This way, we can remove unnecessary tasks from our workload that may not contribute to our specific path. Being mindful of the work we do and how we do it can make a significant difference.

Optimise

By definition, the word optimise means to make the best or most effective use of (a situation or resource). To optimise our work and processes, we need to do what we do really well. We need to start incorporating elements of ideation into our daily routine. What does this mean? It means taking the time to observe and analyse the situation within our team, department, or company and identifying areas where our skills can add more value to the team and have the most impact on the company's goals and objectives. These are the areas we should focus on. Start generating ideas on what you can bring to the table and how you can implement changes in the work being done.

However, it's important to think ahead and consider long-term solutions rather than just quick fixes for workplace challenges. We need to become our own leaders. Once we have a list of ideas, we should prioritise them based on their importance and potential impact. An evaluation tool can help in this process: Analyse the benefits versus the effort required for each task. If a task requires significant effort but offers minimal benefits, it can be deprioritised. Conversely, if a task promises significant benefits with minimal effort, that should be the focus.

By now, you should have a list of changes, tweaks, suggestions, or improvements that you can bring to your workplace. These will make your work more engaging, exciting, and challenging, without feeling the dreadful Monday blues every day of the week.

These need not be major overloads! They can be as simple as:

- Auto-responding to emails and moving them into folders for easy access.
- Creating a presentation template that the whole team can use.
- Simplifying the process taken to solve a customer issue.
- Gaining a certification.

Anything that makes work easier, faster, and saves resources. It's important to prioritise these projects and identify the ones that offer the greatest benefits. Look for projects that you can work on independently, without heavy reliance on others. The idea is to create a proof of concept for the proposed idea. When you can demonstrate the viability of your concept through a small project, it becomes easier for your manager to accept and consider making changes. This is particularly effective when introducing new tools or suggesting simple workflow changes that can enhance efficiency. Implement your ideas, test them out, and if they prove successful, that's great. If not, learn from the experience and move on to the next idea.

Some companies embrace this concept, like Google giving employees a day to work on their own projects or hosting brainstorming sessions where people are allowed to work on projects apart from their regular work. Google is one out of a million companies! Not all companies provide us with the opportunity to work on extra interests or side projects while performing our regular work. Therefore, it becomes our responsibility to create these opportunities for ourselves.

We can allocate small pockets of time to work on these side projects. When we optimise our work and become more mindful, we can dedicate as little as 20 minutes a day or an afternoon each week to our projects and pursuits. That is not so bad!

Initially, these projects may not yield immediate additional results or directly impact our salary or growth. However, they serve as foundational building blocks for our career growth and alignment.

You might think that all of this additional work adds more stress to an already demanding job. However, my dear friends, what we fail to see is that this work challenges us to think outside the box and gets us excited. Working on something new and exciting is far more enjoyable than mundane and uninteresting tasks assigned to us. When you're enthusiastic about your work, you'll find ways to make it happen, and time will no longer be an excuse. Ultimately, you'll become more productive because you're focusing on meaningful tasks that align with your objectives, rather than simply carrying out others' agendas or engaging in tasks that don't contribute to your bigger life goals.

Implementing Systems

Need ideas for big-impact projects to undertake? Implement systems! What are systems? Systems are a set of principles or procedures according to which something is done; an organised scheme or method; different pieces that we can put in place for work to be done smoothly. For instance, if you frequently generate reports from data, implementing a reporting system or utilising project management software can significantly streamline and automate your work. If you manage a long list of client databases, you can benefit from CRM software or integrated systems. There is a cost involved many a time, and if the system can justify how much revenue impact it can have, it is worth consideration.

When it comes to implementing new systems or processes, it's important to approach it strategically. Start by exploring the available options and conducting thorough research on different software or tools that align with your specific needs. Consider the pros and cons of each option and conduct mock runs or trials to test their suitability for your work or department. This initial testing phase will help you identify any issues or areas for improvement before expanding the implementation. This effort also works as a Proof of Concept, which can be used to convince stakeholders for the full-fledged implementation of the system.

Once you have tested and validated the system, involve a beta group of users. This group can consist of a few individuals or a representative sample depending on the project size or nature of work. Seek feedback from this group to gather insights and make necessary adjustments or refinements to ensure the software meets the requirements and expectations.

Before rolling out the system on a large scale, it is crucial to obtain buy-in from all stakeholders. Engage with other departments or teams to ensure their needs and concerns are addressed. Getting support and agreement from all parties involved will increase the chances of successful implementation and adoption.

While it may be tempting to assume that everything will run smoothly once the system is rolled out, it's important to consider the learning curve. Understand that different individuals will require time to familiarise themselves with the new system and may have questions or suggestions along the way. Be patient, provide appropriate training, and offer support to ensure a smooth transition. Monitor the efficiency and effectiveness of the system and make adjustments as needed.

Only when you see that it has been well accepted and everyone has settled into it and the system is used the way it was intended to, can you take a step back and let others handle the implementation further. Don't bring new ideas and systems and leave people hanging with it. This shows your true leadership.

Learning

By now, I am sure the idea of you needing to learn how to do your work differently or better has been drilled into you. Learning is essential for your development. Learning at workplaces can include:

- Learning about systems that help you be efficient at work,
- Learning to master the key tools that you use daily,
- Embarking on more in-depth certifications and higher studies.

It can be something as simple as Excel or PowerPoint or any other software that you are using daily or want to use. Start mastering these tools and equip yourself with the inbuilt features of each tool to utilise them to their fullest.

Many companies offer periodic training or provide scope for you to pursue certifications or degrees that help you grow in your job. If your company is a large corporation, they would have an HR team or an L&D team that works on creating a training calendar for the year where you can opt-in to different appropriate training. But if that is not an option, or if your manager or circumstances do not allow you to take it up at work, bring your own learning plan. Things can be learned even outside of work. We have access to almost every learning portal possible at the tip of our fingertips. Keep upgrading yourself, keep learning new skills and tools that help you Ace at work, and stay updated on the new technologies that are emerging. These will also help you generate new ideas of your own and learn about the innovative ideas being developed by professionals worldwide in your sector or field.

As a final note for this chapter, I want to emphasise an important aspect: amidst all this additional work, changes, tweaks, and optimisations we bring into the workplace, do not lose yourself. It's easy to get consumed by work and let it dominate our lives, occupying the majority of our thoughts. Stay mindful of this and remember the work you did in the previous chapters, where you laid out the foundation for your path.

Chapter Summary

In this chapter, individuals are encouraged to focus on tasks that truly matter, laying the bricks for fulfilling work that gets noticed.

Overall, the key takeaways from the chapter are:

1. Setting clear expectations with stakeholders is crucial for success at work. Clarify goals, objectives, targets, KRAs, and KPIs to know your performance metrics.

2. Get to know what truly matters by paying attention to the bigger picture.

3. Prioritise tasks and projects based on their alignment with company priorities and senior management involvement through open discussions.

4. Optimise your workload by identifying and reducing non-critical tasks and focus on areas where your skills can add value and make a significant impact.

5. Think long-term and focus on solutions that can transform the workplace.

6. Implementing systems and processes strategically can streamline work and improve efficiency. Explore options and research different systems, conduct mock runs, and get buy-in from stakeholders.

7. Continuously learn and upgrade skills to stay relevant in your field.

The key message is to align your work with key objectives (said and unsaid), leverage personal skills, prioritise meaningful tasks, and take ownership of your career growth. Your value isn't derived from just doing your work, but from going that extra mile.

In the next chapter, you will learn how to approach your work so you can make time to work on critical tasks and projects that will further your career.

Check-In Exercise

At this point in the book, take a moment to check-in with what you take away from this chapter.

1. *How is your performance evaluated at your work?*

2. *How do you rate your performance levels at work on a scale of 1 to 10 (10 being the highest)?*

3. *What will you do to increase your score by 1?*

Try the following:

- *Learn about the performance indicators used at your work.*
- *Identify ways to optimise your current work.*
- *Identify opportunities to implement systems and processes at work.*

Chapter Nine

Get Replaced

> *"The only real battle in life is between hanging on and letting go."*
>
> *–Shannon L. Alder*

This may sound counterintuitive, and I am pretty sure an alarm went off in your head!

Won't I lose my job if I do that? Let me take the liberty to remind you that it is only a matter of time before you lose your job. Why am I saying that? Because we are all essentially cogs in a machine. For most work that we do, you can easily be replaced by anybody else. If you are working on some structured, routine tasks in your work, anybody else put in your position with a little bit of training would also be able to do exactly that. If what you bring to the table isn't necessarily what is unique about you, it is only a matter of time before you get replaced. This is why it is so important for us to bring our whole selves and our skill sets into the work that we are doing. Moreover, we don't even need anybody else to replace us. We could, by all means, be replaced by robots with new inventions and technologies around every corner.

With the looming threat of AI taking over our jobs, it is only a reminder for us to relook at our work. If a robot can do your work, then you are not needed! This may be hard to hear, but it is true! I urge you to consider this in a positive frame of mind. Let the robots replace you! Let your routine, structured parts of your job be done by the robots!

Technologies such as artificial intelligence are basically tools that can actually simplify a lot of our work and even help us do our work better and faster. Emails, meetings, reports, and all such tasks are more administrative in nature, and a lot that the robots can help in. While they are necessary, sometimes they are not your potential or your main focus. They are not the tasks that are going to help you Ace at work and fast-track your career growth and advancement. We explored this in detail in earlier chapters, and hence I am hoping you get the flow of thought by now. It is imperative that we become proactive ourselves, and before the robots replace you, get yourself fired. Well, not literally. What "get replaced" means is to free up your time from non-significant activities or activities that are not essential for your career path. Free up your time from these monotonous tasks or things that have been going on the same way forever. When you stop doing these routine activities, your job will become less boring or stagnant, and you will feel more fulfilled because you will then actually be working on tasks that you want to work on and those that matter.

Streamline Workflows

What are workflows essentially? Workflows are the different steps or handshakes that happen for any particular work to get done. When we talk about streamlining workflows, what we essentially need to do is break down the work that is done around you or the work that you do into simple steps and define what goes into these steps. Then look at every opportunity to simplify and optimise the workflow.

The way to start this step is by identifying and implementing your workflows and documenting them. I'm not talking about saying, 'As discussed with you on the phone, I will wait for your reply.' This is documentation in a negative sense. What should you document? You should document SOPs (Standard Operating Procedures) and processes. These are step-by-step guidelines that anybody can read and understand how work is done. These are procedural actions that need to be taken for an output.

Let us understand this better with an example. A simple workflow is how a leave request is processed. Let's say there are three steps in this workflow:

1. An employee needs to raise a leave request in the company's portal.

2. Request approval by the manager.

3. Approval by HR.

It is fairly simple for a small team or company. However, in large organisations, there would be multiple levels of approvals and timelines expected at each level.

A more complex example is in a call centre set-up.

1. A customer raises a complaint.
2. This is logged in their system by an agent and assigned to a specific team.
3. A representative of each team will look at the tickets assigned to his team and assign them to the concerned staff member to investigate.
4. The staff member then studies the issue raised, does routine sanity checks, and either fixes the problem if it is in his capacity or forwards the request further to another team member who needs to take a specific action.
5. If there is an issue, then a change request needs to be raised, and then a different set of processes follow to fix the issue.

This is a very simplified version of the entire story. The point is to actively become aware of the way work gets done. And document it! Large corporate companies would have specific documentation practices and guidelines already set-up. But if you work in a company that doesn't have them, then even better because this is something tangible that you can work on. Like everything else we do, make sure the workflows you are documenting and optimising are ones that you are actively involved in already at your work and that matter or can be automated.

Documentation can also take the form of recording changes and updates. If you're in IT, for instance, you could document the different bug fixes you have done, why you had to do it, and what was the fix that you implemented. You can document your comments alongside the code you are writing so that people who come across it in the future know why a certain line of code was written or corrected.

```
int main()

{

printf("Hello World"); //To display the text in quotes on the screen

return 0;

}
```

This example may be an oversimplification, but if you are following this flow of thought, the idea is to make work easier not just for yourself – fewer questions about what you are doing and why, but also making it easier for anybody else who will take your place. In the future, you can spend less time explaining your work, training new employees, and onboarding new members into your team. Anytime a new employee joins your team, instead of you sitting and training them, you can hand over a set of documents that can be read to catch-up with the work. These documents also help make training very easy, along with onboarding. They also become a repository of all knowledge within the team, and they're an absolute game-changer if people suddenly leave your company or if you don't necessarily want to have a knowledge drain and start from scratch again. They can be used as ongoing training material for different people in the team. Spend all this time saved on those dream pet projects!

The biggest help they can provide is during handovers, especially making it easier for you to take leaves. Someone can be ready to handle your work in your absence even during any unscheduled leaves! I can't emphasise this last one enough!

I once had to handle the work left by a teammate who, due to a health emergency, could not come to work for a week. Needless to say, as this was unplanned, no formal handover or information was given to me. It was a torturous time! I had to figure out everything myself. It was more stressful, and work was severely affected. It was only for a week, but the impact of missed deadlines, tasks that slipped through the cracks, and delays lingered on for months to follow not just for me, but for my teammate once she returned to work too. Such things can affect the entire team and the functioning of the team.

You can make a difference and showcase teamwork and collaborative thinking when you get around to executing these kinds of initiatives. More appropriately, these documents also become your legacy. Even after years, every person who joins your team will read the onboarding document with your name printed on it. You would be in the minds of people even long after your tenure in the company or leaving the job. That is a nice feeling to have!

Further, we need to look at how we can simplify these workflows and processes that we have identified (or documented). For instance, let's say you have identified that there are too many handshakes that happen for a particular task. There are too many levels of approvals, and too many people involved, and it can be very complicated or not clearly understood. Can a 5-year-old understand it? If not, then it is probably something that can benefit from your attention.

We then look at how we can eliminate any unnecessary steps. Identify things that don't add value to the overall task. We can also look at how we can make these processes simpler by modifying them to make everybody's life easier. For instance, it saves time and energy not to wait for a senior manager's approval every time an order has to be placed. It makes things faster. If a small change of waiting for approval can save you 1 day in a project, it means you can complete projects 1 day sooner, thereby increasing the turnaround time of projects. For discussion's sake, let's say each project takes 1 week to complete. This little tweak in the process saves 1 day per project, amounting to 52 days in the year. That is almost 7.5 weeks! What does this mean? You or your team can work on 7.5 additional projects in a year! Thereby increasing the revenue of the company! If all projects cost the same, this translates to 7.5x revenue! Now, you tell me, will your manager object to increasing the revenue by 7.5x?

Furthermore, you can look at the different responsibility areas of who is holding what responsibility in the entire workflow, and we can delegate any of the responsibilities that can be done by others. We will talk more about delegation a little bit later in this chapter. However, know that things can be delegated to other people to simplify your overall workload as well. Swimlane diagrams are great ways to document this.

What we are essentially achieving is making our work faster and simpler. When you do this, we increase the turnaround time of our deliverables, thereby indirectly impacting the company's revenue and creating more cohesive workflows where people are aligned to a common objective. You don't need to be a manager to do that! Hence, helping streamline workflows that you or the others work on will save you a lot of time and help make bigger impacts in the organisation you're working for. As a bonus, such projects can be fun for you too, and a break from your routine work.

Templatise

Templates are basically reusable resources that can be utilised repeatedly. Something that serves as a model for others to copy, such as a preset format for a document or file. Any task that is performed frequently or periodically can benefit from being templatised. This means creating a standardised template for that particular type of work, so you don't have to start from scratch every time. A commonly observed practice of templatising can be found on social media. If you pay attention while endlessly scrolling through social media, you'll notice that many posts from the same person tend to have a similar structure or outline. It is evident that they have been templatised in their work.

A few tweaks to a template like in the diagram above, and the same can be used to create multiple posts quickly and efficiently. Templates reduce reinventing the wheel every time and help speed up work.

What templates do you create? If you work in marketing, then, of course, create templates for social media posts, captions, content calendars, types of posts, etc. In any other field of work too, there is plenty of scope to templatise. These could be in different forms, such as Word documents, PowerPoint presentations, Excel templates, PDF documents, checklists, flowcharts, and swim lane diagrams. Reports that need to be sent out on a daily or weekly basis, status reports for projects, requirement documents, presentations, and standardised emails—these are all examples of things that can be templatised.

How can you create templates? Firstly, start by creating outlines or placeholders for edits. For example, create an outline of a daily report and leave gaps for the information that needs to be updated every day. You could create a PowerPoint presentation template for your project report with all the slides already designed. You just update the graphs, images, or words as needed. Secondly, create repositories of readily accessible elements that can be inserted into your reports, presentations, or emails. Email templates, with standardised formats, can be beneficial for drafting consistent emails. Meeting agendas can also follow a template, ensuring consistency and efficiency. Templates help individuals align with a standardised approach. Once people are accustomed to using templates, it simplifies your and everyone's work because there is no need for second-guessing or deliberating during execution—it becomes a smooth flow.

Automation

Now let's delve into my favourite thing ever! Automation! Here is one mindset that you can adopt and will drastically change the way you work – If something is done more than twice, it needs to be automated. What is automation? Automation refers to the process of reducing or eliminating human intervention in a series of steps. It can be achieved through the application of technology, programs, robotics, or processes. Examples include auto-responders for emails, automatic analysis of data, automated test cases, and scheduled posting on social media. These tasks can be automated using the built-in features of various technologies. Here are some examples of how we can leverage technology's capabilities to automate our work in daily life:

Email Automation: You can set-up auto-replies, move emails into specific folders, schedule emails to be sent, and so much more in any email software you use. Advanced use could include chatbots or robots that can read, summarise emails, and even send automatic replies.

Task Managers: If you use a task management tool, there are plenty of automation options available. You can set-up automatic task assignments for specific individuals based on predefined criteria, update task status, reschedule tasks with dependencies, and so on.

Spreadsheets: If you frequently work with Excel or Google Sheets, you can automate reporting and analytics using features like Excel macros or Google Scripts. There are endless possibilities of how we can utilise these functionalities.

Meeting set-up: Tools like Calendly or other appointment-setting software can ease the setting of individual meetings. Instead of going back and forth about your availability for a meeting, Calendly links or shared team calendars can be used to check when someone is available and block their time.

This is just the tip of the iceberg! Automation can vary from simple tasks to the use of advanced robotics! Many routine tasks can be easily automated using simple solutions and only need a little bit of creativity. With the advent of advanced technologies powered by AI, a lot of our routine tasks can be eliminated or at least simplified. I would not be doing justice if I didn't bring up ChatGPT or Bard! These have essentially reduced a lot of the work we can do! Unless you are living under a rock, you would have heard about these tools and the changing landscape of work. The most surprising use case of ChatGPT that I came across is writing code for Excel macros and SQL scripts. My mind was blown. Spend some time learning how to make the most of these tools. You will not be disappointed. Remember, AI has the potential to replace you. Scratch that! A person who knows how to use AI has the potential to replace you sooner!

Delegation

Delegation is a crucial aspect of our work that can greatly contribute to streamlining workflows and increasing efficiency. I, like a lot of people, hesitate to delegate tasks. One common concern is the fear that delegating tasks to others will make the process more difficult. This reluctance stems from the belief that I can complete tasks faster or better myself. But being able to delegate has freed up so much of my time!

It's important to remember that just because you can do something doesn't mean you should. If a task doesn't necessarily require your unique skills or expertise, it makes sense to delegate it to someone else who can benefit from the opportunity to learn and grow.

Delegation is also sometimes perceived as a loss of control. This is egoistic behaviour and can hinder personal and professional growth. It is essential to recognise that delegation isn't about you losing control but knowing that you can empower others and create growth opportunities for you and those involved.

Delegation is one skill I believe will help you tremendously in making time for all of your focus work. It is a skill, mind you, and is not about pawning off work to others. Let's explore some more nuances of delegation.

When delegating, carefully consider who is best suited for the task. You cannot simply pass on any task to anyone without considering their capabilities and interests. Choose individuals who can benefit from the responsibility and provide them with the necessary skills and authority to accomplish the task effectively. It may be time-consuming at first but will benefit everyone in the long run. Be mindful of the workload of the person to whom you delegate tasks. Overloading someone can hinder their performance and impact overall quality.

Clearly communicate your expectations and provide detailed instructions to ensure a shared understanding of the task at hand. Delegable tasks can include:

- Small-level approvals
- Report preparation
- Meeting agenda creation
- Any tasks that you have templatised or automated.

Delegation fosters skill development, collaboration, and shared responsibility. It allows you to focus on high-priority tasks that require your expertise while enabling others to grow and contribute to the team's success. Effective delegation is a key ingredient in maximising your productivity. You needn't wonder where you will get time to implement the various ideas in this book.

Chapter Summary

By embracing systematic approaches, you are changing the nature of your work. You can work on things that matter to you and the company and feel fulfilled. Becoming an Ace at Work is then a byproduct only indicated by your career growth.

Overall, the key takeaways from the chapter are:

- Jobs are at risk of being replaced, either by more skilled people or by automation and AI, and it's essential to focus on tasks that are unique and irreplaceable.
- To improve efficiency and job security, individuals should bring their whole skill set to work and embrace technology as a tool to simplify tasks.
- Documenting workflows, including SOPs and processes, helps make work more efficient and aids in onboarding and training.
- Streamlining workflows involves simplifying processes, eliminating unnecessary steps, and delegating tasks.

- Templatization can be used for tasks that are performed frequently, reducing the need to start from scratch each time.
- Automation, from email auto-replies to more advanced solutions, can save time and increase productivity.
- Embrace delegation as a means to develop skills, empower others, foster collaboration, and increase overall productivity. Delegate tasks to others when it makes sense, considering their skills, benefits, and relevant authority.

Conceptually get replaced in doing tasks that hold you back from exploring your true worth. Free up your time to work on critical projects and make everyone's life around you easier. Ace at work by doing things differently. Your job is not under threat, you are a threat!

Check-In Exercise

At this point in the book, take a moment to check-in with what you take away from this chapter.

- *How do you feel about getting replaced at work?*
- *How do you rate your leadership skills on a scale of 1 to 10 (10 being the highest)?*
- *What will you do to increase your score by 1?*

Try the following:

- *Find ways to automate your repetitive tasks.*
- *Identify workflows that you can simplify at your work.*
- *Identify templates you can create and tasks you can delegate.*

Final Thoughts

"Winners are not those who never fail, but those who never quit."

–Edwin Louis Cole

I was a workaholic! Today, I feel proud to say that. Not because I believe it is a badge of honour, but because it has taught me so much. When we have the drive to work and work well, we control our growth. For the longest time, I went to work and did what I was told, and that managed to get me where I went.

But, knowing now what I do and implementing the practices mentioned throughout this book has helped me feel good about the work I was doing. It changed my relationship with my work.

A lot of things shared in this book have come from my own experiences at the various jobs I have held. A lot of it is from learning from my colleagues while I was in the roles of a Software Developer, Relationship Manager, or Project Management Analyst. The concepts of relooking at work and drilling down the 'what matters' have helped me maintain my sanity even when all hell broke loose – whether in a job or my entrepreneurial journey. I am not perfect! I have no intention to preach. Many of these concepts I learned a little bit too late. Knowing this earlier would have certainly reshaped my career trajectory. Even today, they continue to help me change the way I work.

When I look back, I see that the most memorable, momentous moments at work have been when I did something out-of-the-box. Reducing the manual effort in checking for missing invoices with the use of a barcode scanner. Using scripts to reduce testing times drastically by automating large test cases. Excel macros have saved the day for me so many times, I lost count. Sending customised emails to over 300 recipients or generating massive reports with analytics in a single button! I am not a tech wizard! But these things happened!

The funny part is that nobody ever said this was my work. It wasn't part of my job description, nor was it discussed in appraisal meetings. But things like these are what got me noticed. Every 'extra mile' I went, more than reaping any financial benefits, made me feel great about my work. It was when I wasn't doing these that I was burning out, feeling stuck, or losing steam.

It was when I wasn't clear about where I was headed that made me fluster the most! This book has been a way for me to rethink what I have been doing! It has helped me clarify what I want to be doing! It has helped me carve time for it. The key that made all the difference for me is to question it all! My work, my desires, my dissatisfactions!

I still am a workaholic – I love to work and want to do more of it! But I now know that burning out while doing it is not a wise option. Prioritising it over everything else – family, friends, health, mental peace, and ourselves – is not just detrimental but is a waste of a life! We don't have enough time to be doing work that doesn't light our souls on fire!

I hope this book has helped turn some wheels in your heads on how you could do things differently. Even doing only a few of the exercises outlined in the book will help change your perspective. That much I am sure of. I have seen my clients transform their lives! One client went from a stressful job to navigating a successful job change, all while pursuing higher studies. Another client mentioned to me that he started saying no more, learned to prioritise, and was looking forward to work. A client effectively managed his workload and got more done in his job even with a side business running! But across the experiences, everyone felt more fulfilled in their lives, even outside of work.

Such results don't come from dreaming. They don't come from drastic changes either. They definitely don't come from just hopping from one job to another. They come when you start to Ace at work. Become Aware, make small changes, and Excel at what you do!

The concepts shared in this book helped me turn my life around. And I sincerely hope it will for you too! Actually, I don't hope so! I know it will! Have seen it happen too many times to believe it is coincidence or luck or destiny. The power to accelerate your career growth, to have a harmonious work and life, or to have a fulfilling, meaningful career, is with you!

What will you do with this power?

It could be realising you were in a career that suits you best. It could be realising that you need a drastic career transition. No one except you knows what you want. Become aware! Choose to not settle but make your dream career a reality!

I would love to hear your experiences about implementing things from this book. Don't forget to check out the free resources that come along with this book at, www.performatbest.com/books/resources. Write to me at peggy.performatbest@gmail.com or DM me on social media handles @performatbest and share your experience. It is not only for me to know how the ideas have impacted you but also to inspire others about the possibilities. It all fuels the mission to empower the entire workforce to have fulfilling meaningful relationships with work itself.

As you go into your work next and Ace at work in your own way, I suggest taking the reflections from this book with you. You will look at your work with a fresh set of eyes! Something switches on inside of us when we do that!

Go be an Ace!

Cheers,

Peggy

About the Author

Pragnya Peggy Venigalla

Pragnya Venigalla, or Peggy as she is lovingly called, is a Certified NLP Practitioner & Coach, Consultant, Trainer, Keynote speaker, and with this book, an Author. She is a passionate individual, a mother, a mentor, and has a zest for life that keeps her wanting more.

Her love for speaking and leadership led her to acquire the coveted Distinguished Toastmaster title, as an active member of Toastmasters International. She is also a proud member of PSAI (Professional Speakers Association of India).

Her keen interest in psychology, processes, & progress directed her from being an IT professional to becoming a Performance Optimisation Specialist, exploring the world of peak performance and productivity! Her background in Engineering, Business Management, and Operations, and her love for learning and development she believes led her down this path.

Having trained, coached & mentored over 1000 people and spoken at various forums and summits, she is looking to create a greater impact by changing people's relationships with their work!

Pragnya is on a mission to help improve the world by helping mid-career professionals convert stressful and stagnant jobs to happier, fulfilled, meaningful careers!

You can reach out to her at peggy.performatbest@gmail.com or visit her website www.performatbest.com.

www.ingramcontent.com/pod-product-compliance
Lightning Source LLC
LaVergne TN
LVHW041036150826
845672LV00001B/344